Timothy W. Downey

with:
Melissa Downey
Catherine Kavanaugh
Gabe Downey

The
Legacy

Honor Flight Michigan

C Moon Publishing
Huntington Woods, MI
www.cmoonproductions.com

Executive Editor: Heidi Press

Associate Editors: Melissa Downey and Joann Beste

Art Director: Jeff Winegar

Concept: Timothy W. Downey

Copy Editor: Jessica Downey

Production Management: University Lithoprinters
4150 Varsity Drive
Ann Arbor, MI 48108
800-652-9414

Print/Production Coordinator: Deborah Sulkowski

Cover and Content Design: Jeff Winegar

Cover Photo: Brad P. Ziegler

Content Photos: Brad P. Ziegler and Nate Strong

Additional Trip Photos: Charles Bovair, Edward Burkhardt, Dave Cameron, Mike Ceaser, Sharon Champine,
Bill Crouch, Mike Culverhouse, Gabe Downey, Debi Hollis, Dennis Martineau,
Marge Schaefer, Ryan Streveler and Chris Zimmel

Portions of the proceeds from the sale of this book go to benefit Honor Flight Michigan.
Quantity discounts available for educational institutions and non-profit or civic organizations.

To contact the author: Timothy W. Downey
c/o C Moon Productions
10734 Borgman
Huntington Woods., MI 48070
248-506-5107
email: tim@cmoonproductions.com

www.honorflightmichigan.com
www.cmoonproductions.com

Printed in Ann Arbor, Michigan – United States of America

ISBN: 978-0-578-07776-5

Since 2006, nearly 1,400 Michigan World War II veterans visited the World War II Memorial in Washington, D.C. which was erected to honor the service and sacrifices thousands of individuals made for our country some 60 years ago. When it was time for their Honor Flight, our home-state heroes had the opportunity to experience first-hand a heartfelt "thank you" from a grateful nation and a caring community. These all-expense-paid, one-day trips were a direct result of the efforts of a few amazing men and women who were board members and volunteers for Honor Flight Michigan.

This book tells the story and confirms the legacy of Honor Flight Michigan. Inside these pages, you will find a chronicle of every trip, including the trip rosters and pictures, stunning photographs of the World War II Memorial and Arlington National Cemetery, as well as many other points of interest. You will read the stories of those who saw that the mission conceived by Honor Flight Michigan founder, the late Dave Cameron, was carried out without a hitch.

This is a story of what a few ordinary people can do when they answer the call – to preserve the memory – and the legacy – of those who so valiantly served our country and preserved our freedoms.

— WITH LOVE AND APPRECIATION —

I would like to sincerely thank all of the following for their many contributions to this book.
Without your help, enthusiasm, support and kindness we would be looking at empty pages. – Tim Downey

Brad P. Ziegler and **Nate Strong** – *Official Honor Flight Michigan Photographers*
If a picture is worth a thousand words, then nowhere is it more evident than on the pages of this book. The sincere commitment and tireless dedication you both have to our World War II heroes and for Honor Flight Michigan are evident in every single photograph. Your photographs speak volumes and are a treasure for the veterans, their families and future generations so that they can relive these amazing Honor Flight trips through your eyes.

Heidi Press – *Executive Editor*
Thank you for all you did to help bring this book to life. I am sure it makes your Dad very proud.

The Honor Flight Michigan Board Members
Margaret Mead once said: "Never doubt that a small group of thoughtful, committed people can change the world. Indeed. It is the only thing that ever has." Thank you for giving me the privilege of serving with you these past few years. You are all amazing, and I am proud to call each and every one of you my friend.

Jeff Winegar – *Art Director*
You took my vision of this book and brought it to life. For that I will be forever grateful.

Dave, Robin, Rachael and **Lily Wojta, Judy** and **Jake Stirnemann** and family, **Jeremy Press, Adam** and **Scott Majors, Jessica Carmichael, Abbie Stark, Auntie Phyllis**, *my new son-in-law* **Brian Luther** *and his family and all my extended family, friends and neighbors.*
I appreciate all you did, whether it was attending or volunteering at fundraisers, being guardians on trips, folding mailers, calling veterans, donating money or just offering a word of encouragement. Thank you for helping Honor Flight Michigan succeed.

Rick Sage and **Pam Robbins**
Rick – What an amazing job you did when you took over Honor Flight Michigan. I am proud to call you my friend.
Rick and Pam – Thanks for all your help in gathering the rosters and other information so valuable in the preparation of this book.

Barbara and **Sam "Red" Press** – **Wilfred** and **Cora Downey**
I would like to dedicate this book to the four people I know best from The Greatest Generation.

My father-in-law, the late Sam Press, was a decorated World War II hero who was quietly proud of his service to our country and one of my personal heroes. To my mother-in-law, the late Barbara "Bubbie" Press, thank you for teaching me how to make everyone's favorite latkes.

To my late father, Wilfred "Papaw" Downey, I can still hear your softly spoken words of encouragement, support and love. I miss you.

To my dear mother Cora Downey, the treasure of our family, I love you and I will be over Sunday morning for breakfast. French toast?

Melissa Downey, **Jessica Downey** and **Gabe Downey**
The gifts of unending support, thoughtful criticism, creative thinking, true kindness, shared happiness, total devotion, a lifetime of laughter and real love – I get all I need from the three of you.

— FOREWORD —

The history of America and of every American is a story of epic scale. For many, these two stories are intertwined with parents, grandparents or great-grandparents participating in World War II. On Sunday morning, December 7, 1941, the Japanese attacked the United States at Pearl Harbor. The first wave of deadly force included 183 planes followed by 167 more and then midget submarines. When the attack was finished, 21 of the 96 ships at anchor had been sunk and others severely damaged. Forty-seven percent of the planes at Hickman, Wheeler and Bellows Airfields had been destroyed and many more damaged. A total of 2,400 soldiers were killed and the wounded exceeded 1,100.

That unprovoked attack ignited the spirit of a generation. It is the boys and girls who were 18 years old in the early 1940's that became the Greatest Generation, won a war, fathered a new generation and built a prosperous nation. It is those boys and girls who 60 years later became the reason for Honor Flight Michigan.

In 2004, the World War II Memorial in Washington, D.C., was dedicated to the men and women who fought against evil and saved the world for democracy and liberty. It is a tribute to those who served, that so many people worked together to establish Honor Flight Michigan. I am inspired by their actions to take care of our American heroes and recognize the patriotism of the Greatest Generation.

Our veterans answered the call for love of country, protection of others, and to fight for their buddies. Honor Flight Michigan answered the call for love of country, for homage to others and to respect these veterans who had sacrificed so much.

Our veterans went to foreign lands at great personal cost. Honor Flight Michigan volunteers went off spending days away from family at great personal cost. The volunteers would say that what they did was a small payment on the debt owed to the World War II veterans. Both groups would tell you that the journey had a profound impact on their lives.

Honor Flight Michigan reminds all of us to make an effort to say "thank you". We need to say that to our veterans and to the generation of men and women who are serving today.

The memorial is solid, impressive and inspiring. The effort of those 18-year-old boys and girls was the same. I salute Honor Flight Michigan, our veterans and their families, and the Greatest Generation. To them I say, we have not forgotten..

Carol Ann Fausone
Brigadier General (retired)
May 2011

— INTRODUCTION —

My association with Honor Flight Michigan is one of the most important and meaningful experiences of my life. I am grateful to have been a board member, guardian, co-trip leader and to have had the chance to spend several Saturdays with 35 to 40 of our most treasured American heroes. To talk with them and walk with them through the grounds at the monument erected to honor their unselfish service to our country is an opportunity for which I will be forever grateful.

To see the many emotions — sorrow, joy and then pride — fill their eyes when they first enter this hallowed ground is a privilege I wish for everyone.

To be selected to serve on the Honor Flight Michigan Board of Directors was a life changing experience for my wife Melissa and me. To work alongside this most caring, kind, considerate, dedicated and amazing group of everyday people whose simple goal was to say "thank you" to nearly 1,400 Michigan World War II veterans has left us both forever humbled and proud.

We now have the pleasure of calling each and every board member dear friends, and all of us will be forever bound together by this unique organization called Honor Flight Michigan. I am sure I speak for all the board members when I say the pleasure of serving these men and women, Michigan's true heroes, was all ours.

Our mission, springing from the idea of our late founder, Dave Cameron, and carried out by a dedicated group of volunteers, is a story in which I am proud to have had a small part. Our goal with this book is to tell future generations what a few ordinary people can do with a common bond and a sense of purpose.

In the following pages you will see the beautiful pictures and read the heartfelt words from all those involved in Honor Flight Michigan. Our beloved World War II veterans, the members of the Honor Flight Michigan Board of Directors, our guardians, our many friends and countless supporters can tell our story much better than I, so I will let each page speak to our history.

This book has truly been a labor of love.

Tim Downey – Author, May 2011

"They fought together as brothers-in-arms. They died together and now they sleep side by side. To them we have a solemn obligation."

– Admiral Chester W. Nimitz

— DEDICATIONS —

The Michigan Honor Flight Board Members
This book is dedicated to each and every World War II hero who Honor Flight Michigan had the distinct pleasure of escorting to Washington, D.C.

We also pay tribute to those soldiers, sailors and airmen who served and did not live to see the World War II Memorial erected by a grateful country.

To Senator Robert Dole, whose tireless efforts in supporting and raising money to build the World War II Memorial will allow future generations an opportunity to remember and say thank you to the over 16 million men and women who served in the Second World War.

To Dave Cameron, our founder and leader. Your moment of inspiration on Sunday morning, September 24, 2006 forever changed the lives of the thousands of people touched by Honor Flight Michigan. May you rest in peace.

Mike Cameron – Honor Flight Michigan Board Member
To the World War II veterans, the Greatest Generation of all time, thank you. This has been a project of love, respect and honor.

Honor Flight Michigan was founded by David and Carole Cameron, my father and mother, to honor a veteran (Carole's father), who was wounded in battle, but chose never to talk about it. As is the case with many veterans, they just did what was asked of them, never looking for praise or thanks.

We can never, ever experience what the World War II veterans lived through, so we cannot understand the sacrifices that were made. The Greatest Generation of this country secured our future as well as the world's future. In appreciation, Honor Flight Michigan was created as a humble attempt to take as many heroes as possible to our nation's capital to see their long overdue, much deserved memorial.

This Legacy of Honor Flight Michigan is for you. Mission Accomplished.

Carol Kavanaugh-Burgess and **Cathy Kavanaugh** – Honor Flight Michigan
To our grandfather – George Rychlinski; Cathy Kavanaugh – To my father-in-law Arnold W. Schwab, Cathy and Carol Kavanaugh-Burgess - To dear friends of our family, Vincent Cutlip, Anthony Cordero and Gustav Gorski; To our great-uncles, William Stark, Edward Podlowski, Albert Rychlinski, Edward Rychlinski and Raymond Rychlinski.

Rick and **Maureen Sage** – Honor Flight Michigan Board Members
Dedicated not only to our beloved World War II heroes, but to all veterans who served this great country, and the memory of those who made the ultimate sacrifice…and in particular, the chance to honor our Michigan World War II heroes through Honor Flight Michigan, keeping Dave and Carole Cameron's vision alive. This major endeavor was the result of an extremely dedicated board, hundreds of donors, volunteers, trip guardians and the overwhelming response from our Michigan World War II vets.

Chris Zimmel – Honor Flight Michigan Board Member
With loving dedication to my dad, Joe Zimmel (Navy). And to my dear uncles, Bill Ong (Army) and Keith Crossman (Navy) – both veterans who sadly passed away without having seen the Memorial dedicated to their service.

Cathy Zimmerman – Honor Flight Michigan Board Member
I dedicate my service to Honor Flight Michigan in memory of my father, Frederick A. Naas, a proud member of the United States Army Air Corps, The 9th Air Force, 397th Bombardment Group, and the 596th Bomb Squadron. I would also like to remember my late husband, Larry L. Zimmerman, and our dear friend, David Cameron. I am privileged to live in this wonderful "Land of the Free" because of the brave men and women who went before me to fight for our freedom. I thank and appreciate those who continue to preserve that freedom today. Technical Sergeant Fred Naas flew 65 missions in B-26s beginning in the pre-dawn hours of D-Day, June 6, 1944 and completed those missions on V-E Day, May 7, 1945. Dad was an engineer gunner, stationed in the top turret of the plane with twin caliber automatic weapons. He was a proud American and an everyday hero.

OUR DEBT TO THE
HEROIC MEN AND VALIANT
WOMEN IN THE SERVICE
OF OUR COUNTRY CAN
NEVER BE REPAID. THEY
HAVE EARNED OUR
UNDYING GRATITUDE.
AMERICA WILL NEVER
FORGET THEIR SACRIFICES.

PRESIDENT HARRY S TRUMAN

MICHIGAN

MISSOURI

Honor Flight Michigan's Inaugural Trip to the World War II Memorial

Saturday, April 21, 2007

— DAVE CAMERON —
Honor Flight Michigan Founder
1938 – 2008

How many of us are touched by a real-life story and moved to help a cause? We click "like" on our Facebook pages, send a check, or if we're real ambitious plan a fundraiser or two.

That wasn't enough for David Cameron after he saw a TV news story about a North Carolina man who took a planeload of World War II veterans to their just-opened national memorial in Washington, D.C.

Cameron was especially moved by the 2006 interview with a former Nazi prisoner of war. The veteran recalled looking from a stalag toward the city of Zagan, Poland, and seeing swastikas come down and U.S. flags go up.

"My wife and I got very emotional when the POW told his story," Cameron said.

They decided every World War II veteran in Royal Oak, Michigan, where Cameron had an insurance business and was active in the community, should have the chance to go. Finally, more than 60 years after the war, there was a tribute to their service and to the 400,000 Americans who made the ultimate sacrifice.

With the blessing of his wife, Carole, Cameron set out to raise $290 for airfare, tour buses, and food for each World War II veteran in the city to go. He organized a board of volunteers to process applications, plan trip logistics, and ask every individual, school, service group and business possible to donate. He set a policy not to accept money from veterans, not even from those willing and able to pay their own way.

"They paid the price, and it's a privilege to do this," Cameron said.

The applications poured in not only from Royal Oak veterans but also from veterans who used to live in the city and veterans across the state who didn't have the money or weren't healthy enough to get to the monument themselves. The board couldn't draw the line at a city limit or county border. That's how Honor Flight Michigan began.

With Cameron's leadership and devotion to veterans, Honor Flight Michigan became the third and most ambitious hub of the emerging Honor Flight Network. Earl Morse of Ohio started the effort, and Jeff Miller of North Carolina followed with chartered flights.

Cameron took the cause to new heights. Honor Flight Michigan became a model for getting veterans, who were dying at a rate of 1,500 a day, to their monument on a regular basis. Some months, the board could afford to send two groups. The board refined the one-day trips, creating a system that could be replicated around the country. Board members found ways to take care of basic needs, like having wheelchairs and box lunches delivered to stops. They trained guardians to help veterans through airport security and around tour destinations, and they added special touches, like greetings by U.S. Senator Robert Dole and a tailored tour of World War II highlights at Arlington National Cemetery.

On the trips, the veterans were overwhelmed at the show of gratitude by Honor Flight Michigan and the strangers who gave them standing ovations at airport gates and posed for pictures with them at the pillars, reflecting pool and pavilions of the sprawling memorial. Many said it was the best day of their life — or at least a close second to their wedding or birth of their children.

Cameron was on a mission to give every veteran in Michigan the hero's treatment.

Catherine Kavanaugh
Honor Flight Michigan Board Member

— HONOR FLIGHT MICHIGAN —

Honor Flight Michigan founder David Cameron devoted the last two years of his life to taking World War II veterans on all-expenses-paid trips to see their national memorial in Washington, D.C. "Every Michigan World War II veteran has earned the right through their selfless service to our state and our great country to see the memorial erected to honor them in Washington, D.C. It is our duty to take them there" he would tell anyone who would listen.

The memorial didn't open to the public until 2004 when the youngest of the World War II veterans were reaching the age of 80. Today, only three million of the 16 million who served are still alive, and they are dying at a rate of nearly 1,500 per day. Time is running out to pay them one last tribute and treat them like heroes again if only for a day.

While watching a CBS news report called "In Their Honor," Cameron and his wife Carole heard the story of Jeff Miller (who would later become Dave's friend) and his efforts to take World War II veterans from North Carolina to Washington to see their memorial. A story by veteran Lt. Joseph Collins, recalling his last day in Stalag Luft 3 in what is now Zagan, Poland, was so moving to the Camerons that they believed they could and should do the same for deserving Michigan veterans, and Honor Flight Michigan was born.

A longtime Royal Oak businessman, Cameron pondered what to do next to get his idea off the ground. He decided to recruit business associates, friends and family members from southeast Michigan to help him with his mission. After creating a volunteer board of directors, his next task was to raise the money to begin the flights. Cameron thought it might take only one or two flights to get all the Michigan World War II veterans who would want to go to Washington, D.C. to see their memorial.

As Cameron shared his plan with the board and the word started to spread, the idea of Honor Flight Michigan quickly became a reality, and the process to seek out the first group of veterans to go to Washington, D.C. began. Cameron and the board members would walk up to elderly men and women on the street and ask them if they served in World War II, and if they would like to take an all-expenses-paid trip to see their memorial in Washington, D.C.

Members of American Legion Post 253, Royal Oak, were among the earliest supporters. Past Commander Bud Wease said some of the post's World War II veterans wept when they heard about the Camerons' mission. They were aware that many veterans could not afford to make the emotional journey or they were not in good enough health to travel alone.

Word spread quickly about this unique opportunity and enough veterans were interested to schedule the first flight. Money to fund the flight was slowly trickling in. Finally, the $25,000 was raised for the first flight, which was scheduled for Saturday, April 21, 2007.

Sixty veterans, eight guardians and their fearless leader Cameron left at 3:30 a.m. from Memorial Park in Royal Oak, Michigan, on luxury motor coaches for a trip to Detroit Metro Airport. With no road map on exactly how to conduct an Honor Flight, Cameron and his group of committed volunteers forged ahead, driven by the opportunity to make a difference in the lives of Michigan's World War II heroes.

The first trip went off without a hitch. "What an amazing, moving experience" many of the veterans were heard to say on the return flight. "Thank you for honoring us and all you did to make this day the best day of my life" a teary eyed veteran exclaimed as he shook Cameron's hand when he got off the bus. Newspapers, television, radio and word of mouth told the story of the successful first Michigan Honor Flight. Cameron and the Honor Flight Michigan Board knew this was the right thing to do. They were more committed than ever to get the word out to every Michigan veteran and let them know of this once-in-a-lifetime opportunity. As Cameron and the board were about to find out, one or two flights might have been a slight miscalculation.

Four years, 33 commercial flights on Northwest and Southwest Airlines and more than 400 luxury motor coach rides later, nearly 1,400 Michigan World War II veterans had taken their Honor Flight. These Honor Flights were supported by nearly 500 guardians who paid their own way for the privilege of chaperoning the veterans to Washington, D.C.

The veterans and guardians enjoyed more than 1,900 bacon-and-egg breakfasts at National Coney Island in Metro Airport. They drank more than 4,000 cups of coffee and 3,000 bottles of water and enjoyed nearly 1,900 Arby's box lunches. They opened nearly 1,400 goody bags containing more than 1,000 digital cameras, 6,000 snacks and candy bars and hundreds of other books and souvenirs.

They attended or participated in more than 70 fundraisers and three reunions. Veterans and guardians visit the Honor Flight Michigan website, www.honorflightmichigan.com, at a rate of nearly 200 per day. There, they can view close to 5,000 pictures highlighting every trip, and each veteran has hundreds of memories of their Honor Flight. Miscalculation may have been an understatement!

Sadly, about 18 months after Honor Flight Michigan was up and running, Cameron's health began to deteriorate. The board and those close to Cameron knew what an undertaking running Honor Flight Michigan was, and all were concerned that the stress contributed to his failing health. Cameron, however, wanted the board to forge ahead. Electing Rick Sage, a retired Royal Oak firefighter and longtime Cameron friend, to continue leading Honor Flight Michigan after Cameron's passing on June 8, 2008 at age 69 was the decision that ensured the continued success of the organization. It was also the occasion to honor the memory of Dave Cameron.

Cameron's obituaries across the state acknowledged what this pioneer of patriotism had accomplished with Honor Flight Michigan. "Cameron's respect for the sacrifices made by World War II veterans knew no bounds. Not only did he lead a volunteer board to raise money to take these veterans on free trips to see their national memorial in Washington, D.C. he did everything he could to make the experience pleasurable and memorable. They literally saved the world," Cameron always said of World War II veterans.

According to Earl Morse of Ohio, who launched the Honor Flight Network, Cameron helped lay the groundwork that made it easier for other states to establish their own groups. Cameron formed the third hub in the United States to take regular trips to the memorial. He also set up one of the most ambitious schedules of the 31 states offering honor flights.

"Because of Dave's success, other people saw this can be done anywhere," Morse said. "To this day we are in awe of him. In an area that is one of the most economically depressed in the country, Dave overcame the financial challenges to make these trips happen." Morse also said he was impressed at how Cameron made a special effort to recruit minority veterans who hadn't heard yet about the effort. "Word about that got to General Colin Powell," Morse said of the former U.S. Secretary of State and retired Army general who regularly greets veterans at the memorial along with former U.S. Senator Bob Dole. "Dave opened the door to that."

Senator Dole called Cameron's family after the Honor Flight Michigan founder died. He talked to Carole Cameron, who had encouraged her husband to start the group, and their son, Michael. "He said it was because of my dad's persistence that he started greeting veterans at the memorial, and now he makes a point to be in Washington, D.C. on Saturdays when the groups from Michigan and other states go," Michael Cameron said.

Dave Cameron's inspiration made a difference in the lives of hundreds of World War II veterans. His selflessness, respect, patriotism, devotion and enthusiasm gave life and breath to an organization dedicated to ensuring that those who fought and survived and those who died protecting our country received the proper recognition for their efforts. He was a quiet leader, dedicated to the cause of giving honor where honor is due.

Dave's legacy and the legacy of Honor Flight Michigan is assured by the thousands of supporters, donors, volunteers, business people, community leaders, civic organizations and his hand-picked board of directors who understood Dave's convictions and sense of purpose and carried out his vision. As Dave would say "because it is just the right thing to do."

And so, it is our honor to pay tribute to this tireless visionary who gave so much of himself for those who gave so much for us.

03:00 - Saturday
Veterans Check-In — Memorial Park, Royal Oak

05:00 - Saturday
Board the Buses to Metro Airport

06:00 - Saturday
Breakfast at National Coney at Metro Airport

07:00 - Saturday
Our Flight Leaves Metro Airport

09:00 - Saturday
We Arrive in Washington, D.C.

10:00 - Saturday
Arrive at the World War II Memorial

A Day in Our Lives

13:00 - Saturday
Our Visit to Arlington Cemetery

14:00 - Saturday
Visiting the Iwo Jima Memorial

IN·HONOR·AND·MEMORY
OF·THE·MEN·OF·THE
UNITED·STATES·MARINE·CORP
WHO·HAVE·GIVEN
THEIR·LIVES·TO·THEIR·COUNT
SINCE·10·NOVEMBER·1775

THE HERITAGE OF
THE UNITED STATES AIR FORCE
AND ITS COMBAT CAMPAIGNS

15:00 - Saturday
Visiting the Airforce Memorial

AERONAUTICAL DIVISION OF THE U.S. ARMY SIGNAL CORPS

15:30 - Saturday
Guided Tours around Washington, D.C.

16:00 - Saturday
Group Photo as We Prepare for the Trip Home

20:00 - Saturday
Arriving Home to Family and Friends

A Day in Our Lives

"Welcome to Meijer's!" exclaimed the elderly gentleman inside the entrance to the store. "Thank you," I replied. That was the third time that particular day I had heard that greeting from the store employee. The only thing different this time was that I was wearing sunglasses. I tried to be incognito as I was entering the store for the third time that day to return cans and bottles. The limit per day was $25.00 and I had almost exceeded it.

Month after month I would return to Meijer at least three times a week to return the bottles and cans I had collected. I had read about an organization in Royal Oak, Michigan, that was sending World War II veterans to Washington, D.C. so that they could see the memorial that was dedicated to their service. The organization, Honor Flight Michigan, was in need of money, and I knew I could help. My father was a proud, brave, patriotic person and decorated American soldier who fought and was wounded in World War II. I felt that raising money for Honor Flight Michigan would further honor my father.

The idea seemed easy. I printed flyers asking my neighbors to leave their returnable cans and bottles on their porches on a designated day. I would leave the flyers in their doors and a few days later I would drive around and pick up the donations. One month turned into two, and before I knew it I had been collecting for six months. In the end, I had returned 30,000 bottles and cans. My proudest moment was handing over $3,000 to Dave Cameron, the founder of Honor Flight Michigan. I knew my donation would allow 10 veterans to make the trek to Washington, D.C.

Dave Cameron saw a dedicated fundraising person and asked me to join the board of directors. That was one of the proudest days of my life. It was Cameron's passion that pushed me to raise as much money as I could to help him reach his goal of sending every Michigan veteran on an Honor Flight. Cameron was a quiet, reserved man. I would meet him in his office with ideas for fundraisers, and I could tell that my enthusiasm overpowered him.

I would suggest dinner dances, magic shows, auctions and more. I know when I started mentioning licenses for liquor, entertainment contracts and room rental fees, he was lost. Graciously, he left all the details to my husband, Tim, and I, and we, along with our wonderful friends on the board delivered every time. Cameron did not need to know every detail of an event.

Grassroots is the key word when I think about Honor Flight Michigan fundraising. If it had not been for the community, many of our fundraisers would have been understaffed and underfunded. Just one article in a newspaper describing an upcoming fundraiser and a need for people to volunteer and others to attend would bring an onslaught of willing people.

The fundraisers were many – auctions, pancake breakfasts, a comedy night, poker nights, and my favorite, A Magical Night for Honor Flight. This fundraiser was held at the UFCW (union) Hall in Madison Heights, Michigan. The evening was made up of an auction of more than 100 items, a catered dinner, dessert, a 50/50 raffle, the sale of Honor Flight merchandise and a lavish show by magician, Arden James. The veterans and their spouses loved the magic show as it was very visual and they did not have to strain to hear dialogue. We ate dinner and held the auction in half of the hall while the show was presented in the other half. Every part of the evening took place under one roof.

Pronto restaurant in Royal Oak was a huge supporter of Honor Flight Michigan. The father of Bill Thomas, one of the owners, is a World War II veteran. We were invited by Bill and his partner Jim to set up a table in the lobby of their restaurant on various patriotic holidays. We sold flags on Flag Day and took donations on Veterans Day. Each time, Bill and Jim encouraged us to hang pictures throughout the restaurant so that diners could understand why we were there. They put placards on tables and even allowed us to sell raffle tickets. Pronto would always donate a giant gift basket or two to auction off. In addition, Bill and Jim would donate a portion of their sales for the day. We were very fortunate to have such generous people helping us!

As with any organization, raising money is always a challenge. Raising money for Honor Flight Michigan, to send our Michigan veterans to Washington, D.C. was a challenge that was very rewarding. At one point I sent a letter to 400 Michigan businesses and private citizens asking to help send our veterans to the national

Fundraising

memorial. I received donations from three companies, two in Michigan and one in California. I saw the advertisement for Esurance on the wall at Comerica Park while attending a Detroit Tigers game and decided to write. Esurance donated $5,000. Quite an accomplishment during my first year on the board!

The bulk of the monies raised came from the community. Veterans, families of veterans, friends, military organizations, Boy Scouts, Girl Scouts and schools were very instrumental in helping us raise funds. They held car washes, bingo games, bake sales, penny drives, The Royal Oak Restaurant Association Mardi Gras fundraiser and more. One business even instituted "casual Friday" whereby employees would pay to wear jeans on Friday with all proceeds going to Honor Flight Michigan.

Schools and school organizations were amazing. We had schools that donated thousands of dollars and others that would donate far less. A teacher in Hazel Park called to tell me that her school had collected money for our cause. There was to be an assembly and she asked if I would come in and talk to the students (K-5). She said the community was suffering as a whole because of the recession and that the students and their parents were not able to donate large sums of money. I wrote a program that could be understood by the students and explained who we were and what we did. The kids sat and listened wide-eyed while I explained that their Grandpas were brave soldiers that fought in World War II. Our photographer, Brad P. Ziegler, brought along large photos of veterans, airplanes used during the war and of the memorial in Washington, D.C. At the close of the assembly the principal presented me with an envelope. Inside was a check made out to Honor Flight Michigan in the amount of $87.63. My voice shook and my eyes teared up as I thanked the group knowing that the sacrifices they made to raise those funds would be almost the cost of a third of a flight for one lucky veteran.

I have a firm belief that each person is put on this earth to help at least one other person. As an Honor Flight board member it was my pleasure to help as many veterans as possible by raising funds to keep the program going until each Michigan veteran was able to witness the beautiful memorial in Washington, D.C. firsthand. My biggest regret is that my own father never made the trip. He would have loved it and been so proud. Each time I went on an Honor Flight surrounded by all of the special World War II veterans, it made me feel just a little bit closer to my father and for that I am grateful.

My resume reads that I graduated from college, shows my work history and all of my volunteer experience. For the past 30 years I have volunteered for a child's organization and a pediatric cancer organization at a local hospital and have been involved in many other fundraising endeavors. The one that brings me the most pride, however, is Honor Flight Michigan. The veterans, my fellow board members and all of the wonderful people I have met in the last four years have made me a far better person. A special thank you to Dave Cameron for taking on this wonderful project, to Rick Sage...there are no words to describe your humility, determination and kindness – you are a forever friend!

To my fellow board members I owe a gigantic thank you for encouraging all of my crazy ideas and jumping in to help me see them to fruition. To my husband, I cannot tell you enough how much I love, appreciate and admire you. And last to my father, thank you for making me see good in all people, thank you for making me realize that it takes a mere second to make someone feel good and thank you most of all for the kind of soldier you were in and out of the war.

Melissa Press-Downey
Honor Flight Michigan Board Member
Fundraising Coordinator

World War II Memorial

Designed by Friedrich St. Florian

Opened to the public on April 29, 2004, the World War II Memorial honors the 16 million American people who served in the armed forces of the U.S., the more than 400,000 who died, and all who supported the war effort from home. Symbolic of the defining event of the 20th Century, the memorial is a monument to the spirit, sacrifice and commitment of the American people. The Second World War is the only 20th Century event commemorated on the National Mall's central axis.

HERE IN THE PRESENCE OF WASHINGTON AND LINCOLN, ONE THE EIGHTEENTH CENTURY FATHER AND THE OTHER THE NINETEENTH CENTURY PRESERVER OF OUR NATION, WE HONOR THOSE TWENTIETH CENTURY AMERICANS WHO TOOK UP THE STRUGGLE DURING THE SECOND WORLD WAR AND MADE THE SACRIFICES TO PERPETUATE THE GIFT OUR FOREFATHERS ENTRUSTED TO US: A NATION CONCEIVED IN LIBERTY AND JUSTICE.

BATTLE OF THE BULGE

MARINE CORPS

ORLD WAR II MEMORIA

GEORGE W. BUSH
PRESIDENT OF THE UNITED STATES

PACIFIC

TARAWA

ARMY AIR FORCES

CHINA · BURMA · INDIA

ST. LO

THE WAR'S END

INS ARE SILENT, A GR

NAVY

Arlington National Cemetery

Located across the Potomac in Arlington, Virginia, Arlington National Cemetery is home to the remains of thousands of military veterans and national figures. Veterans of all the nation's wars from the American Revolution through Iraq and Afghanistan conflicts are buried here. According to Arlington National Cemetery fact sheet, more than 300,000 people are buried here.

Iwo Jima Memorial
Designed by Felix de Weldon

The Iwo Jima Memorial, also known as the U. S. Marine Corps War Memorial, honors the Marines who died defending the United States since 1775. The Memorial is located near Arlington National Cemetery, in Arlington, Virginia, just across the Potomac River from Washington, D.C. It was inspired by a Pulitzer Prize winning photograph of the flag raising by five Marines and a Navy hospital corpsman that signaled the successful takeover of the island. This was one of the most historic battles of World War II. Iwo Jima, a small island located 660 miles south of Tokyo, was the last territory that U.S. troops recaptured from the Japanese during World War II. The capture of Iwo Jima eventually led to the end of the war in 1945.

UNCOMMON
VALOR
WAS A COMMON
VIRTUE

Memorials and Memorable Sites

Officially established in 1965, the National Mall and Memorial Parks actually protect some of the older parkland in the National Park System. Areas within this premier park provide visitors with ample opportunities to commemorate presidential legacies, honor the courage and sacrifice of war veterans, and celebrate the United States' commitment to freedom and equality. The National Mall and Memorial Parks include the following icons: the National Mall, Washington Monument, Thomas Jefferson Memorial, Lincoln Memorial, Franklin Delano Roosevelt Memorial, World War II Memorial, Korean War Veterans Memorial, and Vietnam Veterans Memorial.

— HONOR FLIGHT MICHIGAN —
AN OPPORTUNITY

It is a common belief that opportunity knocks once, and somehow, most of the time we miss it. I am not sure if that is true or does opportunity constantly knock and we just aren't listening?

Maybe we can't hear the knock because we are occupied with other more important things in life, like our busy schedules, commitments, jobs, hobbies, vacations, socializing, scheduling our downtime or dealing with our worries and fears. Could it be these distractions that keep us from hearing when opportunity is knocking on our door?

Opportunity presents itself in many ways and can make us ponder how we might benefit when the knock finally comes. Will it be a chance for a better job, to get rich or be somebody famous? Will it bring happiness, notoriety or fame? Will it change our lifestyle or our circle of friends?

In 2007, opportunity knocked on the doors of a few ordinary people, all at the same time. It was disguised as a State Farm Insurance Agent named Dave Cameron with a dream he called Honor Flight Michigan. Dave spoke of how he wanted to take every World War II veteran from Michigan on an all-expenses-paid trip to see their memorial in Washington, D.C. He said it was our obligation to get them there, and it was their right to see the memorial because of their selfless and heroic service to our country all those years ago.

Dave unveiled his plan explaining how he needed a board of directors to help him raise the funds, plan the trips, book the tickets, order the food, arrange the ground transportation, schedule wheelchairs, order oxygen, buy plenty of bottled water, pack the veterans' goody bags and recruit volunteers as guardians for the flights to help protect and serve our World War II veterans for the entire trip. And by the way, the guardians had to pay their own way.

As one of those ordinary people, soon to become an Honor Flight Michigan Board Member, it sounded more like a full time job than an opportunity of a lifetime to me. But Dave was so committed, I felt compelled to help, and a little arm twisting from my wife and future fundraising director Melissa didn't hurt.

With every worthwhile opportunity comes hard work, and it was part of the equation to be on the board of Honor Flight Michigan. No one knows the amount of hours over the last few years that this dedicated group put in to ensure the success of Dave's Dream. No one counted because everyone could be depended on to do their jobs, even more so after we lost Dave.

Early on, I don't think any of us on the board realized this was the opportunity that would forever

change our lives, but it always felt like important and special work. We were so busy with the trips and fundraisers, that we didn't realize this opportunity was making us all rich beyond our wildest dreams.

This wealth we were accruing, however, was being paid in a different kind of currency, one more valuable than gold or silver. It is a kind of human currency, old as man himself. Instead of dollars and coins by which we would normally measure riches, we were being paid with a heartfelt thank you, warm hugs, firm handshakes, grateful tears and moving letters of appreciation. We were being paid with human kindness, these days a rare and precious commodity that can never be devalued or lost in the stock market.

A familiar quote says "you get more than you give." These humble, gracious veterans who we had the pleasure of escorting on their Honor Flights are all shining examples of this truth. They repeatedly suggested we were doing so much for them, when in fact it was they who were doing so much for us—the board, the guardians, the fundraisers and volunteers of Honor Flight Michigan.

Dave Cameron would say these veterans earned their Honor Flight more than 60 years ago with their selfless service to our country when we needed them most. When they heard opportunity knock in the early 1940s, they did not spend a lot of time contemplating their fate or being concerned about their future well-being. They weren't wondering "what's in it for me" or about how much of their precious time the call to duty would rob them of their remaining years. No, these heroes, our heroes, heard opportunity's knock and flung open the door. And each and every one of us owes them a debt of gratitude we can never repay.

We must recognize that each opportunity presented to every American in every aspect of our lives since the end of World War II is absolutely a direct result of the service and sacrifices these 16 million ordinary American citizens—men and women alike, including the more than 416,000 who laid down their lives — made for us and indeed for the world. We must never forget.

It was in that spirit and in their honor that the board of Honor Flight Michigan pledged to do its job, and to that I humbly say: Mission Accomplished.

This journey we call life often offers us the privilege of opportunity and places upon us the responsibility to give something back by becoming more than what we used to be. Dave Cameron and Honor Flight Michigan afforded all of us involved just such an opportunity—an opportunity to say "thank you" to nearly 1,400 of our beloved World War II heroes, an opportunity to admire the work of almost 600 guardians and countless volunteers and supporters who were vital to the success of our missions. An unknown author once wrote "Those who can, do. Those who can do more, volunteer." Fitting words to describe all those involved with Honor Flight Michigan.

To Dave Cameron, our inspiring and amazing World War II veterans, our guardians, the many volunteers, my fellow board members and to my amazing wife Melissa who introduced me to Honor Flight Michigan, please accept my sincere thanks for the gift of Honor Flight Michigan. I will cherish it always and the opportunity you all gave me to be more than I used to be.

Tim Downey – Board Member, Author

Honor Flight Michigan Board of Directors

— RICK SAGE —
Board Member — Executive Director

Thanks to my dad's World War II reunion group, I've come to love, honor and respect that Greatest Generation! My dad and mom used to go to his reunions every year, and when my mom passed, my dad still wanted to attend. I took the time off of work from the Royal Oak Fire Department and escorted him and even hosted a reunion in the Detroit area a couple of years before he died. These heroes "adopted" me and even invited me to attend their reunions after my dad passed, which I looked forward to every year. But the sad thing is missing the ones who had died prior to the ensuing year's reunion.

Then, in the fall of 2006, my good friend Dave Cameron, asked me to join him in his quest to follow Honor Flight National's idea of escorting World War II veterans to Washington, D.C. to visit their memorial. An extremely dedicated Honor Flight Michigan Board was initiated, money raised, and trips planned starting in the spring of 2007. Thirty-three trips and almost 1,400 heroes later, Dave's vision became a reality. It was a great honor to be elected to take Dave's place as Director when he passed. I vowed to make it MY quest to, in Dave's words, "Git 'er done!"

I've read every single application, and to this day I am in awe at the accomplishments of these courageous men and women, what they went through and the fact that they made it home! I served in Vietnam, spending a year in the jungle, with all that it entailed, and know some of what those guys went through, but it still boggles my mind.

It really is difficult to describe the emotions that well up inside me when I recall all the work that went into this wonderful, intense, fulfilling endeavor. It was the most worthwhile project I've ever been involved with. The thanks (handshakes, cards, calls and emails!) our passionate crew and I would receive after a trip made it all worthwhile. These humble men and women were astounded at the reception they'd receive at the airport and all during the trip, having strangers, especially school kids, shake their hands and thank them for their service. Although they are receiving it late, they are finally getting the overdue appreciation they so justly deserve.

God bless our veterans!

Rick Sage

— MAUREEN SAGE —
Board Member

I became involved in Honor Flight Michigan when I met and married my husband, Rick Sage, another Honor Flight board member. I not only gained a husband, but also a wonderful Honor Flight family when I married Rick. I was thrilled to become involved with Honor Flight, helping with applications, mailings, and donations, along with anything else that needed to be done.

Honor Flight Michigan has forever changed my life.

First and foremost, it allowed me to meet and work with a phenomenal group of individuals. They will always have a place in my heart. I have learned through them a great deal about dedication, hard work, and believing that it can be done if you have a vision. I experienced a fine example of teamwork.

The most wonderful surprise was meeting the veterans. Being privileged to go on three flights, I was in awe of the humble, proud and patriotic men and women who served in World War II. Serving their country was a privilege to them, and as a group, they were so unassuming, brought to tears by the cheering crowds at the airport and by the young students who were so happy to meet a true American hero.

My most memorable moment came on my second trip. We had assembled at Arlington Cemetery for the Changing of the Guard. There were many wheelchair-bound veterans on that trip, and we made sure that they had front row seats so they could see the ceremony.

One veteran sitting next to me in his wheelchair was very crippled by arthritis and complications from a stroke. A very delicate gentleman, I thought. But when they started playing "Taps," that soldier struggled to stand up, and with a tear rolling down his cheek and a proud look in his eye, he saluted his flag and his countrymen, then slowly sat down in his wheelchair and wiped away his tear.

Maureen Sage

— BRAD P. ZIEGLER —
Board Member — Official Photographer

E ver since I was a cadet at Valley Forge, I felt the desire to be a part of a group, some sort of fraternal organization, a "Band of Brothers" if you will. It must be the instilled "Esprit De Corps" that a cadet falls in love with at such an influential age.

After September 11 I was desperate to be a part of the action taking place in the military. My friends from Valley Forge were going to Iraq and Afghanistan. I was angry and scared, but what could a commercial photographer do? The answer didn't come until years later after I had moved to Michigan. I had photographed a piece with my "Flyboys" for Hour Detroit magazine. I introduced myself to Dave Cameron, and he invited me to be on the board of Honor Flight Michigan.

I had found my mission, my contribution and my action of service as my grandfather had years before when the attack on Pearl Harbor came. My service was to help his generation recognize their own service and see their memorial. About 25 missions later I photographed and delivered thousands of images to families and veterans to help them reconcile their past and hopefully bring them enjoyment.

We can't heal old war wounds, but I think we certainly helped bandage them. Honor Flight Michigan is my service and tribute to my grandfather and his entire generation. He joined the U.S. Navy on December 8, 1941. On September 10, I was on the roof of the World Trade Center, the next day was my Pearl Harbor; it just took me a little longer to take action. He was an electrician on the Tuscaloosa, a heavy cruiser, who saw both theaters, Atlantic and Pacific, and went from chasing the Tirpitz in the North Atlantic to the signing of surrender at Tokyo Bay. He was part of something very special.

I was part of something very special that will never be equaled – Honor Flight Michigan.

Brad P. Ziegler

— NATE STRONG —
Board Member — Photographer

I t's a rare treat for anyone to meet his one true hero in life. To spend a fleeting moment in his or her presence is a fortune few are allowed. I've been lucky not only to have met hundreds of my heroes, but also to have spent close to four years physically and spiritually by their sides. More importantly, I was blessed with the opportunity to express my infinite gratitude to so many of them—the World War II veterans who fought, sacrificed and suffered 60-plus years ago all in the name of freedom, freedom that my family and I benefit from every single day. And I have Honor Flight Michigan to thank for it.

While I never served in the military, I am extremely thankful to have served with the amazing people of Honor Flight Michigan. From the board to the guardians and volunteers, I've been extraordinarily privileged to be a part of a group that shared the same passion and devotion that I have. Expressing our love and appreciation to those who did nothing less than save the world, bound us all into a dedicated, enthusiastic, generous and truly unique group. Together, we sent nearly 1,400 Michigan World War II veterans to their National Memorial in Washington, D.C.

Honor Flight Michigan also provided me firsthand history lessons from those who actually made history. Veterans who traveled to D.C. with us also found themselves traveling more than six decades into their past. As they stood before the monument in their honor, they were once again storming beaches, jumping behind enemy lines, surviving kamikaze raids, bailing from bombers, healing the wounded, driving supply trucks and shooting down enemy fighters. I stood next to them as they again battled through Pacific jungles, Italian mountains and European winters. I saw tears as they were liberated from POW camps, laid fallen comrades to rest and struggled with survivor's guilt. Through them all, I was both humbled and honored to have been a passenger on these personal journeys. I was also proud to be a small part of the ultimate result: providing a final and gratifying chapter—a sense of closure—to these unimaginably brave men and women.

These are memories and life lessons I will forever cherish. They also will be passed along to friends, family and future generations in order to ensure that the legacy of our World War II veterans will never be forgotten. The flights may have ended, but this mission will remain with me long into the future and is the inspiration behind wanting to create an educational traveling World War II museum.

Honor Flight Michigan was truly a miraculous gift – a gift of giving. I gave my heart, time, talents, laughter and tears to those who gave their all. Very few things in life make a person feel better than being allowed to give wholly of himself. Having the opportunity to do so for such a noble, worthy and fulfilling cause leaves me eternally grateful.

Nate Strong

— CHRIS ZIMMEL —
Board Member — Medical Consultant

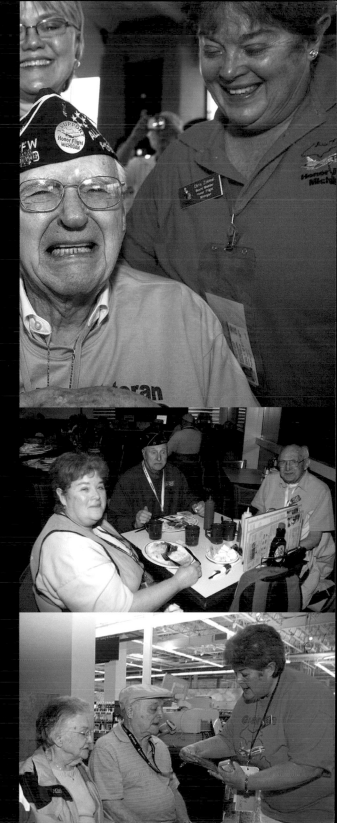

My route to Honor Flight was influenced by my parents. My father, like other young men the day after Pearl Harbor, lined up trying to enlist for military service. However, bad vision did not make him a candidate so he worked in a war defense plant. My mother, a nurse, had a bout with TB and was also ineligible to serve so she worked double shifts to cover for the doctors and nurses who went off to war. Shortly after they were married, my dad's last attempt at volunteering was successful and he was stationed at the Naval Air Station in Hutchinson, KS where my mom worked in a local hospital. My mother's devotion to nursing pointed me in that direction and reading about World War II flight nurses inspired me to become one.

I worked with Carole Cameron (Dave's wife) and she wore an Honor Flight Michigan shirt to a meeting one day. We talked at length about the plans that she and Dave had made for Honor Flight. She discussed my flight nurse experience with Dave and he asked me to join the HFM Board.

As the HFM Medical Advisor, my mission and promise to every veteran and their families was to ensure they were carefully monitored and assisted by qualified medical personnel so that we could "bring them back to their families in the same condition that we received them". I am proud to say that, due to the outstanding efforts of the Medical Guardians, we accomplished that mission.

To guarantee that we were properly staffed, we reviewed the Medical Guardian applications and selected the most qualified individuals. We did a thorough review of each veteran's medical history and often made personal calls to ensure we had the latest information. Companies in the community like St. John Providence Health System and Wright & Filippis loaned or donated equipment for our trips and for that we are grateful.

The Medical Guardian teams often spoke to me after the flights expressing how much they personally got out of the trips. Working with these dear, unassuming veterans, who just couldn't believe that so many people were paying them homage was wonderful. I would like to thank them all for saving the world.

Chris Zimmel

— CATHY ZIMMERMAN —
Board Member — Trip Preparation

It certainly has been my privilege and honor to be a board member of Honor Flight Michigan from its inception in 2006. When Dave Cameron (Honor Flight Michigan founder) called me to ask if I'd like to get "involved" in his latest project, little did I know what was in store for me! Dave was a dear friend, and had done so much for my late husband and my family, there was no way I would or could say no to Dave.

Besides, my dearly beloved father, Tech. Sgt. Frederick A. Naas, was a World War II veteran whose crew flew 65 missions in Europe in B-26s. Dad's first mission was D-Day, June 6, 1944, and he completed those missions by V-E Day, May 7, 1945. Technical Sergeant Naas was in the 9th Army Air Corps, the 397th Bomb Group, and the 596th Bomb Squadron. My father was an engineer gunner in the top turret manning twin caliber automatic weapons. I saw Honor Flight Michigan as an opportunity to honor Dad, and his fellow veterans from World War II.

My father had always shown us it was important to be a patriot, honor our country and stand and salute the flag when it was presented. He was a quiet hero from the Greatest Generation who spoke little of his wartime experiences. In later years friends from his squadron would reveal what a true hero Dad really was in his quest to protect our country. Honor Flight Michigan gives me a chance to give back in appreciation for all that our veterans have done, and will continue to do for our country.

I have never been associated with a more dedicated, attentive, patriotic, unselfish and affectionate assembly of individuals than the board of Honor Flight Michigan. I consider Dave's request to join his group as a true blessing in my life, and I will always be grateful for his invitation. I owe you one again, David Cameron! He left me with the gift of a whole new circle of truly remarkable friends, and a wonderfully rich purpose and dream to fulfill in his memory.

I have met the most extraordinary people through Honor Flight Michigan, and the most amazing World War II veterans. It truly is my privilege to assist the veterans, and my fellow board members. You have all taught me so very much, and please know I appreciate each and every one of you board members and veterans. Again, thanks for the memories…I salute you ALL.

In gratitude and fondly,

Catherine (Cathy) Naas Zimmerman

— CAROL KAVANAUGH-BURGESS —
Board Member

I am the proud granddaughter of World War II Navy veteran, George Rychlinski, and niece to several great-uncles who also served in World War II. Many other uncles served in the Korean War and one earned a Purple Heart and a Bronze Star. In addition, my father was in the Army. My sister, Catherine Kavanaugh, is a fellow board member. I live in Warren, Mich., with my husband, Dennis.

Being a part of Honor Flight Michigan has touched my life so profoundly that it actually helped me become patriotic and understand what that really means. For someone born in 1969, I really took my freedoms for granted even after 9/11. The best moments of all the flights I went on always occurred at the actual memorial. To watch a veteran from Korea, Vietnam or the Gulf War help a World War II veteran get around, and to see a World War II veteran light up from the attention of a current serviceman or servicewoman gave me goose bumps. In their respect for each other I saw a sacred bond.

On the trips veterans share stories, and I felt connected to my grandfather and uncles who passed away never speaking of their experiences at war. All my history lessons were brief snippets from school textbooks. Then, I learned firsthand about sacrifices made. These heroes shared their personal histories and I won't forget them.

It was the easiest most gratifying charity work. I got to spend time with living history. Never a burden, never a chore, never work. It was pure enjoyment.

I am more mature for the adventure of each flight and more appreciative of my freedoms for they were fought for by so many that I now know.

I miss the board members. I miss the planning and organizing. I really miss the flights. I really miss the lessons. I truly miss spending time with the bravest people who literally gave us freedom.

I give my thanks, love, respect and gratitude to all veterans.

Carol Kavanaugh-Burgess

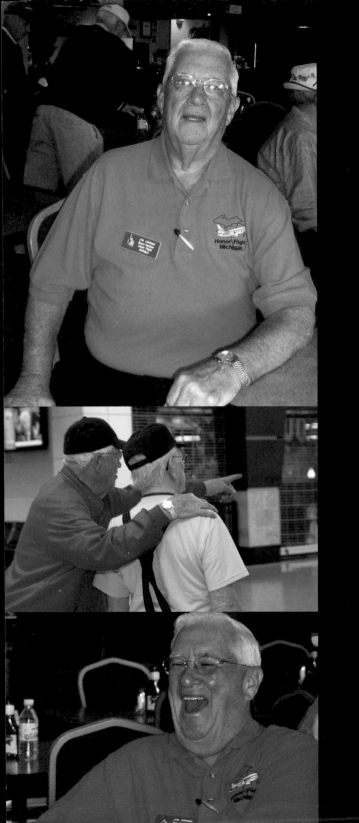

— JIM JOHNSON —
Board Member — C.P.A.

Dave Cameron approached me at the very beginning to help him find a CPA and attorney who would be willing to file for exempt status with the IRS and annual tax returns at a bargain price to help out the expense side of the ledger. We were not able to locate one at a decent price. My son and I decided that our firm is knowledgeable in this type of accounting, and we would offer our services pro bono. He then asked me to sit in at the board of directors meetings in case there were any questions, and I did. After seeing the dedication of the board members and sensing the urgency of the situation I became enamored with the goals of Honor Flight Michigan and soon wanted to become more involved with sending World War II veterans to Washington, D.C. to visit their memorial along with a sightseeing trip for the day.

From the very first trip, I became a member of the "Ground Crew." I checked in the veterans on every trip, made sure all were accounted for, had breakfast with them and got them all on the airplane. I did this for 3 ½ years and was so glad I did. These heroes were so appreciative it sent chills down my spine. Wow! What a group of guys and gals to just meet and be around! I heard stories and quips that were unbelievable. I took one trip to Washington, D.C. with the veterans. The experience was fabulous and even made me more proud to be a guardian of our heroes.

The memories and satisfaction I derived from being a part of Honor Flight Michigan and its dedicated group of individuals has been fantastic, and I will never forget the words: "It is better to give than to receive." Words cannot express the satisfaction I received in exchange for being willing to give of my time for our heroes.

Jim Johnson

— CATHY KAVANAUGH —
Board Member

Because of Honor Flight Michigan, my family now knows precious more about what my father-in-law, Arnold Schwab, went through in World War II. Before the last trip in May 2010, we knew little more than he was an Army medic with the 92nd Field Hospital in the Philippines. He didn't share many details before he died in 2005 at age 80. Five years later, a couple days after the final Honor Flight, we learned so much more.

It all started with a last-minute veteran cancellation. Because my husband, Bill Schwab, was at the airport as "Ground Crew" (helps vets through security, then National Coney Island, then the gate), he got to go on the trip as a guardian with my son, Evan, 6, and me. They were paired up with 87-year-old Navy veteran Ed Milewski, who serviced radar during World War II. Bill and Evan loved every minute of giving all the veterans the VIP treatment. They took pictures of Mr. Milewski at a spot where he could see the World War II Memorial reflecting pool on his right and the Washington Monument on his left. He called his daughter to share the moment.

Bill wished he could have shared the moment with his dad. Eighteen hours later, when we got home, he went online and looked up the 92nd Field Hospital. He found a book on the outfit that became the first Mobile Army Surgical Hospital. One of the doctors had kept a journal of the hospital's construction and operation. Bill ordered two copies. When it came in the mail, he and my mother-in-law couldn't believe what they were holding—a never-seen-before photo of my father-in-law. He is standing with three other shirtless guys and some operating tables. The caption says it's the morning cleanup. The photo is on a page recounting what it was like on one the worst days of patching up U.S. servicemen.

Bill tracked down the author, Dr. John C. Gaisford, and asked if he remembered his father. The doctor couldn't be sure; my father-in-law's 6 foot, 6 inch lanky build seemed vaguely familiar to him. Bill thanked him for writing the book that gives all kinds of glimpses into his father's military life in the spring and summer of 1945. We know what life was like for the servicemen crossing the Pacific on the Noordam and how morale was lifted with a visit from some of the Broadway cast of "Oklahoma". We also know how highly regarded the staff was to Dr. Gaisford. "These boys worked like no others I had ever seen. There was never a complaint. All they wanted to do was to help save the injured."

Because of Honor Flight Michigan, my family—and future generations—now have a better idea of Arnold Schwab's role in World War II and a better understanding of why we are so proud of his service.

Cathy Kavanaugh

— PAM ROBBINS —
Board Member

I have been a resident of Royal Oak, Michigan, for 62 years.

It was the Fall of 2006 when a friend, Dave Cameron, came to me asking my opinion about a show he had watched one Sunday morning. The show was a Charles Osgood show featuring a man, Jeff Miller, who was flying World War II veterans to see their memorial in Washington, D.C.

Dave was asking my opinion on whether I thought we could form an organization in Royal Oak, where we worked and lived, to do the same thing. My thought was, yes we could. Since my own father was a deceased World War II veteran, it gave me the feeling that I could do this to honor him.

Dave started asking for volunteers to be on his board. He had a passion for this project like I had never seen in him before. Just being asked to be included in Dave's organization was an honor. I knew it would be successful. Our mission was to escort our World War II veterans to Washington, D.C. to see their memorial that was recently opened to the public.

All the board members worked tirelessly toward our common goal, and we succeeded. After many fund raisers, newspaper articles and mountains of applications for veterans and guardians we were able to put our first trip together. In April of 2007 we were able to take our first busload of veterans to the airport to fly to Washington, D.C. Every trip was a learning experience. I worked to develop the early website and keep the mountains of data in order for our files and address lists of the veterans waiting their turn to go on the trip of a lifetime.

Giving back to our community in such a positive way was a gratifying experience. Never before had I belonged to such a great group of committed people working together toward a common cause. I made many new and lasting friendships while having to deal with the loss of the friend who started the entire project and never got to see it through.

The loss of Dave Cameron shook our organization to the core, but we continued Dave's work as he would have himself. We completed our mission in 2010, but Honor Flight Michigan will never end for me. It's one of the most cherished memories for me to hold onto for the rest of my life.

To be in the midst of the heroes we honored was one of the best experiences. I could never, ever have imagined this was happening to me.

Thank you Honor Flight Michigan, Dave Cameron and all the board members who made this effort possible and a dream come true to so many.

Pam Robbins

— CYNDY CANTY —
Board Member

I am the proud daughter of the late Milton Bruce, who served in World War II as an Army Corporal stationed in the Philippines. He came home after the war and went on to serve as a firefighter for his hometown of Ferndale, Michigan, a true example of The Greatest Generation.

My involvement with Honor Flight Michigan took root when I became friends with a group of Army Air Force veterans who call themselves "The Flyboys". I served as a guardian on their Honor Flights in June and November 2007, and it was so rewarding. I joined the Honor Flight Michigan Board of Directors in December 2007 and assisted in fundraising and public awareness for Honor Flight Michigan. I accompanied Honor Flights in November 2008 and April 2010 as team leader.

Whether it was highlighting World War II veterans on my radio show, promoting Honor Flight Michigan events, or getting to know the veterans and the other Honor Flight Michigan volunteers, I will always count my involvement with Honor Flight Michigan to be one of the high points in my life.

Cyndy Canty

— MICHAEL McCARTHY —
Board Member — Travel Coordinator

Honor Flight Michigan was an opportunity for me to personally meet and thank the World War II veterans from our state. I was proud to be a part of Honor Flight Michigan and work on behalf of these humble men and women—our World War II heroes.

It was my job and pleasure to be involved with the logistics team for each and every flight. Our responsibilities included flight procurement, ground transportation, reservations, wheelchairs and motor coaches. It was a wonderful opportunity to be able to assist the Honor Flight Michigan board and volunteers in making our Detroit departures and our arrivals in Washington, D.C. a great success.

Every departure was exhilarating, especially seeing the genuine glee and humble gratitude expressed by our World War II soldiers. They were all so pleased to have the opportunity to go to Washington, D.C. to see their memorial. Our Honor Flight Michigan board was instrumental in welcoming and showing our heroes a wonderful and safe time. As the proud son of a World War II Navy veteran, I am proud to have played a small part in our trips and hopefully give something back to those who gave so much for us, especially the gift of freedom. God bless them all!

Michael McCarthy

— KEVIN SUTHERLAND —
Past Board Member — Retired Treasurer

I still get tears in my eyes when I reflect on that first time I heard about Honor Flight. I was having breakfast at National Coney Island in Royal Oak, Michigan at 7 a.m. in October 2006 when Dave Cameron called me over to his table and told me about this television show he had watched on Sunday with his wife, Carole.

The TV show talked about Jeff Miller from North Carolina who wanted to say thank you to all World War II veterans in his county by offering them a free trip to Washington, D.C. to visit the recently completed World War II Memorial which honors all World War II veterans. It took more than 60 years to finally build this monument, and thanks to Senator Robert Dole, it was now completed.

Dave asked, "Why couldn't we get a group together here in Royal Oak to take some local veterans to Washington, D.C. as well." I thought it was a great idea, but how do we get started? After discussing the idea during this breakfast, we decided that all we needed to do was get some publicity to let veterans know what we were going to do and how they could apply, raise money and schedule an airplane trip. It did become a lot more complicated than that (insurance, nurses, guardians, buses, supplies, bank account, etc.), but after organizing a group of our friends to work on this project through the winter of 2006, we finally began sending about 50 veterans every two weeks during the summer of 2007 to Washington, D.C.

I will never forget that first breakfast with Dave and five or six of his friends. Dave Cameron had his dream, and his dream became a reality. How these few people in the Royal Oak area built upon this dream, raised more than $700,000 and eventually sent nearly 1,400 World War II veterans to Washington, D.C. in the space of just four years is the real miracle. My blessing was the opportunity to be a small part of Honor Flight Michigan and to see the tears in those veterans' eyes when they arrived in Washington, D.C.

God bless Dave and Carole Cameron and all World War II veterans.

Kevin Sutherland

— MIKE CAMERON —
Board Member

As a son of Honor Flight Michigan founder, Dave Cameron, I just want to express my gratitude to the wonderful World War II veterans that I've been privileged to meet on our trips. We can never repay the debt we owe them for their service to our country and I am so very grateful for the opportunity to take these heroes to their long overdue memorial in Washington, D.C.

My involvement in Honor Flight Michigan started at the onset when my father said, "I have an idea and I need some help" and so it all started with a spaghetti dinner. Four years later it has come to a glorious finish. I have to say I am truly blessed to have played a small part.

Thank you to everyone involved who helped complete my father's dream. He would be in awe of the accomplishments of Honor Flight Michigan.

Michael Cameron

— JEFF MILLER —
Co-Founder Honor Air

A tribute to my friend... I met Dave Cameron at the Michigan column at the WWII Memorial, April 21, 2007. He had just arrived with the first Honor Flight Michigan trip and was so excited. We had talked many times on the phone but this was our first face to face meeting and the first hug of many to come.

As a co-founder of Honor Air, I advised hundreds of well intentioned people, wanting to take their heroes to Washington, D.C., but most of could never make it happen. In my first phone call with Dave, I knew Michigan would fly. He was a passionate and a detail person. His goal was to make no mistakes and to do it better than anyone else – and he did.

He always give others credit for the success of Honor Flight Michigan and stood in the background. He was comfortable there, watching the faces of these humble heroes beam with pride and happiness in the long over-due realization that they had done something big...they had saved the world.

Dave introduced me to one of my heroes, General Colin Powell, and never let me forget that! We shared many special moments and I grew to love Dave. He touched so many lives with Honor Flight Michigan. He was a true American hero taken from us to soon. I keep his photo on my wall and in my Honor Air lanyard when I visit a veterans group. I am a better man for having known him and I know I will hug Dave again.

Jeff Miller

— DEBI HOLLIS —
Volunteer

Becoming involved in Honor Flight Michigan has been one of the best things I have ever done. I was recently asked what makes me happy. One thing is doing something that makes a difference in someone's life. That's what Honor Flight allowed me to do. Being able to give the veterans their "moment" and watch them experience their joy have given me some of my happiest moments. Their appreciation and gratitude are a lesson for us all. I've been able to develop friendships with some of the veterans I flew with, which is a true gift. They've come to my family cottage on Memorial Day and showed us the real way to celebrate – with those who were there. I take great pride in knowing these veterans. Hearing their stories has given me a firsthand account of history that would have never been possible without Honor Flight Michigan. They truly are the Greatest Generation – through their actions on the trips, they have taught kindness, respect, patriotism, love and friendship. They are full of life, spirit and spunk. What more could someone ask for? We did this for them, having no idea what they would give to us in return. I love them all. My heart is full.

I remember when I signed up for my first flight. I was really looking forward to being a one-on-one guardian and getting to know one specific veteran. Then I found out I was assigned to be a team leader. I was concerned that this would stop me from getting to know the veterans. I'd be too busy keeping track of them all instead! How wrong I was! This was the best opportunity; I'm still in touch with two veterans from that first trip! Then I went on to be team leader one more time and trip leader three times. I once invited all the out-of-town veterans who were staying at the airport to have dinner with me at the airport hotel. We had a group of 13 that night. What an awesome way to spend time with them and get to know them before the chaos of the next day began! I'm still in touch with a few of those veterans too – one of whom lives close to me. I've been to his home for dinner, visited him in the hospital and celebrated with him and his wife at my family's cottage.

I've watched them, full of energy, running in the rain, full of emotion, crying at the airport reception, full of joy, smiling at the crowds, full of patriotism, saluting today's young soldiers, full of respect, watching the Arlington guards change duty, and full of gratitude, giving hugs to the volunteers. Every emotion was shared. Every emotion was shown. Nothing held back. These are the men and women of the Greatest Generation. God bless them all as he has blessed me with their friendship.

Debi Hollis

— DAVE WOJTA —
Volunteer

I have always been influenced by those involved in WWII, including two of my uncles and my father-in-law. They were the inspiration and reason I enlisted in the Marine Corps then spent many years in the Army Reserve and volunteered for Honor Flight Michigan.

On the day of our flight, the buzz of veteran-to-veteran conversations was very familiar to me. Meeting everyone and working to make the trip happen made the day unforgettable. The veteran to veteran relationship transcends all others as those who have been tested by fire have a unique bond.

The memorial is so beautiful and at times overwhelming. When Senator Bob Dole greeted the vets, there were many smiles, photos and shared memories. We toured Arlington National Cemetery and witnessed the changing of the guard at the Tomb of the Unknown Soldier. It was one of the most solemn, awe inspiring hours I have ever experienced and the tears flowed. The quote; "All Gave Some, Some Gave All" was brought to mind by row upon row of white tombstones. As hundreds of these veterans go on to their final duty station every day I am grateful that I had at least a small part in expressing our gratitude to them for a job well done.

Dave Wojta

— DUSTIN RICE —
14 Year-Old Guardian

I am very proud to be a small part of Honor Flight Michigan and to dedicate a day to the brave men and women who served our country in the face of total war. Going on an Honor Flight as a guardian with these men and women to the World War II memorial and then going through Arlington National Cemetery was definitely a chance of a lifetime.

My day was amazing. I will never forget all of the friends that I made and the way the veterans all looked at me when they saw me in the bright orange guardian T-shirt. Several of the veterans put their trust in me very quickly and told me stories that they had not told anyone since the end of the war. These emotional stories will always remain in my heart, and I will honor their wish and keep them to myself.

With the help of my aunt I have been able to stay in touch with many of the veterans. Honor Flight Michigan changed me into a better person, and I know that I have grown from the wealth of knowledge that I have learned from this program.

Dustin Rice

Ralph C. Banwarth	**Herbert A. Doyle**	**James R. Johnson**	**Paul A. Manik**	**Raymond H. Olsen**
World War II Veteran	World War II Veteran	World War II Veteran	World War II Veteran	World War II Veteran
Madison Heights, Michigan	Royal Oak, Michigan	Hazel Park, Michigan	Oak Park, Michigan	Royal Oak, Michigan
Edwin H. Barton	**Bruce T. Flack**	**Thomas L. Joliat**	**Robert W. Matthews**	**Cyril A. Oosterlinck**
World War II Veteran	World War II Veteran	World War II Veteran	World War II Veteran	World War II Veteran
Royal Oak, Michigan	Clawson, Michigan	Royal Oak, Michigan	Rochester Hills, Michigan	Royal Oak, Michigan
Robert E. Benjamin	**George C. Green**	**Kenneth E. Karpinen**	**Miriam Schroff Melvin**	**Bert W. Oxley**
World War II Veteran	World War II Veteran	World War II Veteran	World War II Veteran	World War II Veteran
Royal Oak, Michigan	Royal Oak, Michigan	Madison Heights, Michigan	Royal Oak, Michigan	Clawson, Michigan
Kenneth W. Brancheau	**Henry A. Gruzwalski**	**Lawrence J. Klepack**	**Richard H. Melvin**	**Frederick W. Penney**
World War II Veteran	World War II Veteran	World War II Veteran	World War II Veteran	World War II Veteran
Royal Oak, Michigan	Clawson, Michigan	Royal Oak, Michigan	Royal Oak, Michigan	Royal Oak, Michigan
David B. Braum	**John J. Guirey**	**Edward Kolokoski**	**Roy E. Murray**	**Irvin L. Reed**
World War II Veteran	World War II Veteran	World War II Veteran	World War II Veteran	World War II Veteran
Royal Oak, Michigan	Berkley, Michigan	Lathrup Village, Michigan	Royal Oak, Michigan	Ferndale, Michigan
Donald R. Bush	**Burl W. Harper**	**Harold F. Law**	**Douglas W. Nagel**	**Joseph Rezetka**
World War II Veteran	World War II Veteran	World War II Veteran	World War II Veteran	World War II Veteran
Royal Oak, Michigan	Royal Oak, Michigan	Metamora, Michigan	Madison Heights, Michigan	Royal Oak, Michigan

World War II Veteran
Royal Oak, Michigan

World War II Veteran
Rochester Hills, Michigan

World War II Veteran
Waterford, Michigan

Trip Guardian
West Bloomfield, Michigan

Trip Guardian
Royal Oak, Michigan

Elwood L. Ruffles
World War II Veteran
Royal Oak, Michigan

Joseph L. Villerot
World War II Veteran
Troy, Michigan

Harold F. Williams
World War II Veteran
Royal Oak, Michigan

Larry J. Engel
Trip Guardian
Carlsbad, California

John Wendland
Trip Guardian
Royal Oak, Michigan

Lewis R. Rutledge
World War II Veteran
Royal Oak, Michigan

Robert T. Weinberg
World War II Veteran
Eastpointe, Michigan

Renee K. LeVasseur
Trip Guardian
Clawson, Michigan

Catherine Zimmerman
Trip Guardian
Royal Oak, Michigan

Wilfrid O. Schroeder
World War II Veteran
Clawson, Michigan

Charles E. Weis
World War II Veteran
Berkley, Michigan

David Cameron
Trip Leader
West Bloomfield, Michigan

Beth C. Matter
Trip Guardian
Birmingham, Michigan

Eugene R. Skalsky
World War II Veteran
Troy, Michigan

John F. Wendland
World War II Veteran
Royal Oak, Michigan

Richard D. Ballard
Medical Personnel
Macomb, Michigan

Matthew W. Murray
Trip Guardian
Royal Oak, Michigan

Norman E. Soper
World War II Veteran
Royal Oak, Michigan

Richard L. Westerman
World War II Veteran
Clio, Michigan

Brad P. Ziegler
Official Photographer
West Bloomfield, Michigan

Richard P. Sage
Trip Guardian
Royal Oak, Michigan

Honor Flight 1 Saturday, April 21, 2007
More photos of this trip at www.honorflightmichigan.com

2

George Banda	Frederick E. Haustein	Peter Malega	Ernest J. Scalzi	Wallace R. Wilmot
World War II Veteran	World War II Veteran	World War II Veteran	World War II Veteran	World War II Veteran
Southfield, Michigan	Clinton Township, Michigan	Madison Heights, Michigan	Berkley, Michigan	Royal Oak, Michigan

Thomas J. Dolf	John Horiszny	Gordon T. McEwen	Harry C. Seavey	John T. Wood
World War II Veteran	World War II Veteran	World War II Veteran	World War II Veteran	World War II Veteran
Royal Oak, Michigan	Birmingham, Michigan	Berkley, Michigan	Leonard, Michigan	Rochester Hills, Michigan

Raymond J. Dulecki	Richard L. Humphrey	Richard P. McLaughlin	Steve E. Sendek	
World War II Veteran	World War II Veteran	World War II Veteran	World War II Veteran	
Madison Heights, Michigan	Royal Oak, Michigan	Macomb, Michigan	Royal Oak, Michigan	_____

Dean W. Eggart	George E. Jones	Richard W. Nummer	Frank Sinacola	David Cameron
World War II Veteran	World War II Veteran	World War II Veteran	World War II Veteran	Trip Leader
Troy, Michigan	Royal Oak, Michigan	Chesterfield, Michigan	Royal Oak, Michigan	West Bloomfield, Michigan

Edwin A. Farr	Eugene S. Kaczmar	John Pardy	William E. St. Clair	Elizabeth J. Blaquiere
World War II Veteran	World War II Veteran	World War II Veteran	World War II Veteran	Trip Guardian
Detroit, Michigan	Madison Heights, Michigan	Madison Heights, Michigan	Royal Oak, Michigan	Royal Oak, Michigan

Armond A. Ferrari	George B. Klaput	William Provensha	Robert W. Urquhart	William H. Crouch
World War II Veteran	World War II Veteran	World War II Veteran	World War II Veteran	Trip Guardian
Madison Heights, Michigan	Royal Oak, Michigan	Erie, Michigan	Shelby Township, Michigan	Oxford, Michigan

Clarence E. Gallagher	Henry H. Krug	Gordon E. Rowe	John A. Walford	Robert N. Gajewski
World War II Veteran	World War II Veteran	World War II Veteran	World War II Veteran	Trip Guardian
Northwood, Ohio	Berkley, Michigan	Pontiac, Michigan	Royal Oak, Michigan	Royal Oak, Michigan

Harry M. Grover	Michael E. Larkins	Lytle B. Russell	Regis A. Welsh	John P. Humphrey
World War II Veteran	World War II Veteran	World War II Veteran	World War II Veteran	Trip Guardian
Davisburg, Michigan	Royal Oak, Michigan	Royal Oak, Michigan	Madison Heights, Michigan	Royal Oak, Michigan

Gary May
Trip Guardian
Royal Oak, Michigan

Ayleet "Bud" Wease
Trip Guardian
Royal Oak, Michigan

Michael McCarthy
Trip Guardian
Royal Oak, Michigan

Calvin W. Wilkinson
Trip Guardian
Royal Oak, Michigan

Peg Moore
Trip Guardian
Ann Arbor, Michigan

George W. Nummer
Trip Guardian
Clawson, Michigan

Deborah A. Peak
Trip Guardian
Royal Oak, Michigan

Nicholas J. Phillips
Trip Guardian
Novi, Michigan

Pamela Robbins
Trip Guardian
Royal Oak, Michigan

Richard P. Sage
Trip Guardian
Royal Oak, Michigan

"They have given their sons to the military services. They have stoked the furnaces and hurried the factory wheels. They have made planes and welded the tanks, riveted the ships and rolled the shells."

– President Franklin D. Roosevelt

Honor Flight 2   Saturday, May 5, 2007

3

Norman R. Allaire World War II Veteran Berkley, Michigan	Louis A. Dieckmann World War II Veteran Hazel Park, Michigan	Edward G. Lash World War II Veteran Huntington Woods, Michigan	William R. Palmer World War II Veteran Troy, Michigan	Robert N. Stauffer World War II Veteran Royal Oak, Michigan
Ervin J. Brzezinski World War II Veteran Berkley, Michigan	Cecil E. Donahue World War II Veteran Royal Oak, Michigan	Yvonne V. Linehan World War II Veteran Royal Oak, Michigan	Fred E. Reichel World War II Veteran Rochester Hills, Michigan	Dale A. VanAmberg World War II Veteran Berkley, Michigan
Forrest O. Burtner World War II Veteran Troy, Michigan	Richard C. Fields World War II Veteran Elkhart, Indiana	Thomas E. Lootens World War II Veteran Royal Oak, Michigan	William A. Rosnyai World War II Veteran Bloomfield Hills, Michigan	Clifford VanNest World War II Veteran Royal Oak, Michigan
Calvin E. Burtner World War II Veteran Royal Oak, Michigan	James F. Frenchi World War II Veteran Troy, Michigan	John A. Marsh World War II Veteran Rochester Hills, Michigan	Roland G. Rosslip World War II Veteran Royal Oak, Michigan	Herbert C. VonRusten World War II Veteran Rochester Hills, Michigan
Richard Chavez World War II Veteran Royal Oak, Michigan	John W. Graham World War II Veteran Pontiac, Michigan	Robert E. Meyer World War II Veteran Allen Park, Michigan	Lyle Russell World War II Veteran Berkley, Michigan	——————
Murray A. Cotter World War II Veteran Beverly Hills, Michigan	Ross Jarvis World War II Veteran Warren, Michigan	Walter J. Miller World War II Veteran Royal Oak, Michigan	Wilbur S. Shaffmaster World War II Veteran Royal Oak, Michigan	David Cameron Trip Leader West Bloomfield, Michigan
Robert R. Cunningham World War II Veteran Royal Oak, Michigan	Leonard Johns World War II Veteran South Rockwood, Michigan	John B. Moultrup World War II Veteran Beverly Hills, Michigan	Houghton C. Smith World War II Veteran Royal Oak, Michigan	Dee Hilbert Medical Personnel Rochester Hills, Michigan
James W. Dawson World War II Veteran Royal Oak, Michigan	Robert W. Jordan World War II Veteran Beverly Hills, Michigan	Frederick G. Nunnold World War II Veteran Royal Oak, Michigan	Harry S. Smith World War II Veteran Waterford, Michigan	Brad P. Ziegler Official Photographer West Bloomfield, Michigan

Cynthia Canty
Trip Guardian
Birmingham, Michigan

David Moultrup
Trip Guardian
Beverly Hills, Michigan

Catherine Zimmerman
Trip Guardian
Royal Oak, Michigan

Louis C. Fleury
Trip Guardian
Royal Oak, Michigan

Louis K. Rogers
Trip Guardian
Oak Park, Michigan

Mark Frenchi
Trip Guardian
Clarkston, Michigan

John L. Salter
Trip Guardian
Royal Oak, Michigan

John L. Graham
Trip Guardian
Ortonville, Michigan

Anne V. Scott
Trip Guardian
Royal Oak, Michigan

Robert W. Lucas
Trip Guardian
Dearborn, Michigan

Nate Strong
Trip Guardian
Wixom, Michigan

Harry S. McCabe
Trip Guardian
Ferndale, Michigan

Mark Stutzmann
Trip Guardian
Ann Arbor, Michigan

Richard W. Moore, Jr.
Trip Guardian
Ann Arbor, Michigan

David G. VanAmberg
Trip Guardian
Livonia, Michigan

Richard W. Moore, Sr.
Trip Guardian
Ann Arbor, Michigan

Ayleet "Bud" Wease
Trip Guardian
Royal Oak, Michigan

" Americans came to liberate, not to conquer, to restore freedom and to end tyranny. "

– Inscribed on base of flagpoles at World War II Memorial.

Honor Flight 3 Saturday, June 2, 2007
More photos of this trip at www.honorflightmichigan.com

Donald R. Carter	Lorenzo W. Holloway	Richard D. Macon	Charles P. Ring	Calvin P. Taylor
World War II Veteran	World War II Veteran	World War II Veteran	World War II Veteran	World War II Veteran
Detroit, Michigan	Detroit, Michigan	Detroit, Michigan	Lake Orion, Michigan	Cadillac, Michigan
James C. Doig	Bernard F. Hoste	Richard A. Majoros	Gordon E. Ryan	Donald C. Thomas
World War II Veteran	World War II Veteran	World War II Veteran	World War II Veteran	World War II Veteran
Dearborn Heights, Michigan	Warren, Michigan	Davisburg, Michigan	Troy, Michigan	Detroit, Michigan
H. C. Edwards	Archie Hovsepian	Andrew F. Mitchell	Richard J. Sadowski	Jordan Tiller
World War II Veteran	World War II Veteran	World War II Veteran	World War II Veteran	World War II Veteran
Suttons Bay, Michigan	Waterford, Michigan	Warren, Michigan	Rochester Hills, Michigan	Detroit, Michigan
Robert L. Firman	Adolph E. Hunacek	Joseph J. Mraulak	Albert E. Schoening	James L. Tyrrell
World War II Veteran	World War II Veteran	World War II Veteran	World War II Veteran	World War II Veteran
Commerce Township, Michigan	Ferndale, Michigan	Ann Arbor, Michigan	Ferndale, Michigan	Pontiac, Michigan
Joseph C. Gardner	Louis Kingston	Chester R. Nelson	Leonard Sims	Robert L. Wenzel
World War II Veteran	World War II Veteran	World War II Veteran	World War II Veteran	World War II Veteran
Royal Oak, Michigan	Oak Park, Michigan	Detroit, Michigan	Detroit, Michigan	Southfield, Michigan
Alfred F. Giusti	Leslie F. Knowles	Philip O. Newton	Nora L. Sims	Richard T. Wolas
World War II Veteran	World War II Veteran	World War II Veteran	World War II Veteran	World War II Veteran
Oak Park, Michigan	Waterford, Michigan	Howell, Michigan	Detroit, Michigan	Warren, Michigan

4

David Cameron
Trip Leader
West Bloomfield, Michigan

Lynda R. Grosjean
Medical Personnel
Clarkston, Michigan

Bruce A. Manny
Medical Personnel
Ann Arbor, Michigan

Susan M. Schuldeis
Medical Personnel
Royal Oak, Michigan

Brad P. Ziegler
Official Photographer
West Bloomfield, Michigan

Catherine Kavanaugh
Press - Media
Dearborn, Michigan

Thomas J. Bowker
Trip Guardian
Berkley, Michigan

Frank Gregory
Trip Guardian
River Rouge, Michigan

Jodi S. Manny
Trip Guardian
Ann Arbor, Michigan

Michael McCarthy
Trip Guardian
Royal Oak, Michigan

Andrea L. Mitchell - Alexo
Trip Guardian
Sterling Heights, Michigan

Eugenia M. Mraulak
Trip Guardian
Ann Arbor, Michigan

David P. Neary
Trip Guardian
Royal Oak, Michigan

Charles P. Ring
Trip Guardian
Washington Township, Michigan

Harold J. Robinson
Trip Guardian
Royal Oak, Michigan

Richard P. Sage
Trip Guardian
Royal Oak, Michigan

Anthony C. Sims
Trip Guardian
Detroit, Michigan

Kevin Sutherland
Trip Guardian
Royal Oak, Michigan

" There was never a good war, or a bad peace. "

– Benjamin Franklin

D-DAY JUNE 6, 1944
YOU ARE ABOUT TO EMBARK UPON THE
...T CRUSADE TOWARD WHICH WE HAVE STRIVEN THESE
...NY MONTHS THE EYES OF THE WORLD ARE UPON YOU...
I HAVE FULL CONFIDENCE IN YOUR COURAGE,
DEVOTION TO DUTY AND SKILL IN BATTLE.

GENERAL DWIGHT D. EISENHOWER

Honor Flight 4 Saturday, July 7, 2007
More photos of this trip at www.honorflightmichigan.com

Pius A. Bohn World War II Veteran Oakland, Michigan	**Anthony DiBella** World War II Veteran Warren, Michigan	**Russell Hammond** World War II Veteran Richmond, Michigan	**Russell H. Mayer** World War II Veteran Kingston, Michigan	**Bruce R. Sherman** World War II Veteran Cass City, Michigan
Harold C. Born World War II Veteran Southfield, Michigan	**Burney J. Elliott** World War II Veteran Marlette, Michigan	**Edward W. Hanley** World War II Veteran Wyandotte, Michigan	**Don F. Morell** World War II Veteran Spring Lake, Michigan	**John R. Snow** World War II Veteran Highland, Michigan
Raymond L. Brabo World War II Veteran Oxford, Michigan	**Mitchell M. Figa** World War II Veteran Clarkston, Michigan	**John G. Howell** World War II Veteran Waterford, Michigan	**Delbert E. Morley** World War II Veteran St. Clair Shores, Michigan	**Alan Stefani** World War II Veteran Warren, Michigan
Fidell Cashero World War II Veteran Livonia, Michigan	**Leland D. Fischer** World War II Veteran Marlette, Michigan	**Alexander Jefferson** World War II Veteran Detroit, Michigan	**Arthur E. Neate** World War II Veteran Roseville, Michigan	**Donald E. Steiner** World War II Veteran Oxford, Michigan
John B. Cook World War II Veteran Peck, Michigan	**Albert C. Foote** World War II Veteran Decker, Michigan	**Paul S. Kearns** World War II Veteran West Bloomfield, Michigan	**Robert C. Phillips** World War II Veteran Kingston, Michigan	**John L. Sulich** World War II Veteran Royal Oak, Michigan
Leland A. Cotter World War II Veteran Oxford, Michigan	**Earl V. Fosgard** World War II Veteran Harrison Township, Michigan	**Kenneth E. Kilmer** World War II Veteran Marlette, Michigan	**Daniel Redman** World War II Veteran Deckerville, Michigan	**Kenneth L. Urwiller** World War II Veteran Bloomfield Hills, Michigan

John Widajewski
World War II Veteran
Roseville, Michigan

Melissa Downey
Trip Guardian
Huntington Woods, Michigan

Ayleet "Bud" Wease
Trip Guardian
Royal Oak, Michigan

Judith A. Figa
Trip Guardian
Clarkston, Michigan

Sandra M. Werner
Trip Guardian
New Baltimore, Michigan

David Cameron
Trip Leader
West Bloomfield, Michigan

John R. Frazier
Trip Guardian
Marlette, Michigan

David Wojta
Trip Guardian
Huntington Woods, Michigan

Ofelia A. Neate
Medical Personnel
Troy, Michigan

Joseph Hanley
Trip Guardian
Okemos, Michigan

Rudy Bolf
Trip Guardian
Bad Axe, Michigan

Gary May
Trip Guardian
Royal Oak, Michigan

Charles F. Bovair
Trip Guardian
Novi, Michigan

Michael McCarthy
Trip Guardian
Royal Oak, Michigan

Rodney L. Cotter
Trip Guardian
Lake Orion, Michigan

Edward A. Neate
Trip Guardian
Troy, Michigan

Henry A. Cox
Trip Guardian
Ortonville, Michigan

James J. Neate
Trip Guardian
Macomb, Michigan

"Our debt to the heroic men and valiant women in the service of our country can never be repaid. They have earned our undying gratitude. America will never forget their sacrifices."

– President Harry S. Truman

Honor Flight 5 Saturday, August 4, 2007
More photos of this trip at www.honorflightmichigan.com

Gertrude E. Balan
World War II Veteran
Ferndale, Michigan

Donald G. Garvin
World War II Veteran
Howell, Michigan

Kurt G. Kersten
World War II Veteran
Grosse Ile, Michigan

Burton R. Miner
World War II Veteran
Royal Oak, Michigan

Horatio T. Rork
World War II Veteran
Canton, Michigan

Richard H. Berry
World War II Veteran
Southfield, Michigan

Joseph Guzzio
World War II Veteran
Commerce Township, Michigan

Harold M. Kott
World War II Veteran
Flat Rock, Michigan

Tadeusz F. Muszynski
World War II Veteran
Holland, Ohio

Jesse Rutledge
World War II Veteran
Detroit, Michigan

Willor Brown
World War II Veteran
Ypsilanti, Michigan

William H. Hassard
World War II Veteran
Waterford, Michigan

William C. Larson
World War II Veteran
Shelby Township, Michigan

Hershel H. Myers
World War II Veteran
West Bloomfield, Michigan

John E. Sanders
World War II Veteran
Troy, Michigan

Cornelius J. Cavanaugh
World War II Veteran
Royal Oak, Michigan

William C. Herrmann
World War II Veteran
Farmington, Michigan

Robert B. Lash
World War II Veteran
Utica, Michigan

Alexander A. Opoka
World War II Veteran
Highland, Michigan

Arthur P. Secord
World War II Veteran
Berkley, Michigan

Harry J. Cavanaugh
World War II Veteran
Royal Oak, Michigan

Ramiro Hinojosa
World War II Veteran
Dearborn, Michigan

Donald A. Lorimer
World War II Veteran
Clawson, Michigan

Charles S. Pike
World War II Veteran
Sterling Heights, Michigan

John C. Sirlag
World War II Veteran
Troy, Michigan

Robert G. Cook
World War II Veteran
St. Clair Shores, Michigan

Boleslav W. Jarocha
World War II Veteran
Livonia, Michigan

Cecil R. Luttenbacher
World War II Veteran
Oak Park, Michigan

Chester F. Pisarski
World War II Veteran
Washington, Michigan

John C. Southward
World War II Veteran
Toledo, Ohio

Michael Cyrek
World War II Veteran
Centerline, Michigan

Leo W. Karczewski
World War II Veteran
Redford Township, Michigan

Andrew G. MacGowan
World War II Veteran
Sterling Heights, Michigan

Franklin J. Quinlan
World War II Veteran
Davisburg, Michigan

Robert J. Thompson
World War II Veteran
Toledo, Ohio

Robert H. Dunne
World War II Veteran
Sterling Heights, Michigan

William T. Kenny
World War II Veteran
Huntington Woods, Michigan

Conrad E. Miesiak
World War II Veteran
Troy, Michigan

Robert W. Remillard
World War II Veteran
St. Clair Shores, Michigan

Walter J. Whitmer
World War II Veteran
West Bloomfield, Michigan

Karen Masser
Trip Guardian
Highland, Michigan

David Cameron
Trip Leader
West Bloomfield, Michigan

Michael D. McCarthy
Trip Guardian
Southfield, Michigan

Brad P. Ziegler
Official Photographer
West Bloomfield, Michigan

Margaret J. Monroe
Trip Guardian
Royal Oak, Michigan

Rick Berry
Trip Guardian
Royal Oak, Michigan

Janet Owoc
Trip Guardian
Wixom, Michigan

Bruce E. Garvin
Trip Guardian
Brighton, Michigan

Dorothy Pakulski
Trip Guardian
Toledo, Ohio

Thomas Kowalec
Trip Guardian
Sterling Heights, Michigan

Rebecca R. Paul
Trip Guardian
Westland, Michigan

Karen L. Markstrom
Trip Guardian
Royal Oak, Michigan

Delores Pike
Trip Guardian
Sterling Heights, Michigan

Joel C. Markstrom
Trip Guardian
Clarkston, Michigan

Patricia A. Salter
Trip Guardian
Royal Oak, Michigan

"We are determined that before the sun sets on this terrible struggle our flag will be recognized throughout the world as a symbol of Freedom on the one hand and of overwhelming force on the other."

– General George C. Marshall

Honor Flight 6 Saturday, September 8, 2007
More photos of this trip at www.honorflightmichigan.com

Mario J. Angelo
World War II Veteran
Rochester Hills, Michigan

George W. Busse
World War II Veteran
Royal Oak, Michigan

Harold E. DeForest
World War II Veteran
Sterling Heights, Michigan

Harry E. Hartshorne
World War II Veteran
Northville, Michigan

Robert J. Kippert
World War II Veteran
Macomb, Michigan

Wallace M. Barringer
World War II Veteran
Farmington Hills, Michigan

Thelma M. Cannon
World War II Veteran
Royal Oak, Michigan

Robert E. Dodge
World War II Veteran
Davisburg, Michigan

Eugene M. Haxter
World War II Veteran
Roseville, Michigan

Harvey G. King
World War II Veteran
Rochester, Michigan

Howard H. Behrman
World War II Veteran
Plymouth, Michigan

Michael G. Ceaser
World War II Veteran
Canton, Michigan

Harry R. Easton
World War II Veteran
Roseville, Michigan

Frederick L. Henry
World War II Veteran
Detroit, Michigan

Calvin F. King
World War II Veteran
Rochester Hills, Michigan

Robert J. Bentz
World War II Veteran
Troy, Michigan

William J. Clissold
World War II Veteran
Lake Orion, Michigan

Richard S. Elegert
World War II Veteran
Detroit, Michigan

Donald R. Hill
World War II Veteran
Warren, Michigan

Robert F. Lavens
World War II Veteran
Bloomfield Hills, Michigan

William R. Blaznek
World War II Veteran
Allen Park, Michigan

Leo Coleman
World War II Veteran
Fraser, Michigan

William A. Finley
World War II Veteran
Milford, Michigan

Beryle E. Hines
World War II Veteran
South Lyon, Michigan

David E. Laverdiere
World War II Veteran
Troy, Michigan

John H. Bohrer
World War II Veteran
Royal Oak, Michigan

Valentino Colussi
World War II Veteran
Walled Lake, Michigan

Harold H. Fischer
World War II Veteran
Jackson, Michigan

Glenn H. Jahnke
World War II Veteran
Bloomfield Hills, Michigan

Clarence C. Lephew
World War II Veteran
Ferndale, Michigan

Edward Borkin
World War II Veteran
Wixom, Michigan

Joseph F. Cuddington
World War II Veteran
Commerce, Michigan

Charles F. Gerds
World War II Veteran
Commerce Township, Michigan

Francis W. Keenan
World War II Veteran
Merrill, Michigan

John C. Levick
World War II Veteran
Rochester Hills, Michigan

Donald Bujold
World War II Veteran
Rochester Hills, Michigan

James D. Culverhouse
World War II Veteran
Lake Orion, Michigan

Donald A. Gocella
World War II Veteran
Bloomfield Hills, Michigan

Alvin B. Killeen
World War II Veteran
New Hudson, Michigan

George A. Luenberger
World War II Veteran
Auburn Hills, Michigan

Russell H. McCoin	Mark W. Miller	Ralph G. Richard	Lester Singer	Francis P. Weaver
World War II Veteran	World War II Veteran	World War II Veteran	World War II Veteran	World War II Veteran
Garden City, Michigan	Jackson, Michigan	Lake Orion, Michigan	Berkley, Michigan	Waterford, Michigan
Ralph McGreevy	Alexander G. Miros	John M. Roberts	Joseph A. Staccy	John S. Wells
World War II Veteran	World War II Veteran	World War II Veteran	World War II Veteran	World War II Veteran
St. Clair Shores, Michigan	Sterling Heights, Michigan	Bloomfield Hills, Michigan	Westland, Michigan	Bloomfield Hills, Michigan
Merwin McKechnie	John A. Montgomery	Earl A. Roberts	Robert E. Standfest	Edward E. Werner
World War II Veteran	World War II Veteran	World War II Veteran	World War II Veteran	World War II Veteran
Davison, Michigan	White Lake, Michigan	West Bloomfield, Michigan	Fraser, Michigan	Sterling Heights, Michigan
Donald S. McQueen	Aloysios Nadratowski	Theodore R. Ronk	John A. Starkey	Henry R. White
World War II Veteran	World War II Veteran	World War II Veteran	World War II Veteran	World War II Veteran
Birmingham, Michigan	Novi, Michigan	Jackson, Michigan	Sterling Heights, Michigan	Clinton Township, Michigan
Donald F. Melesky	George M. Olshove	Ted Rzeszotarski	Victor J. Stevens	Floyd V. Williams
World War II Veteran	World War II Veteran	World War II Veteran	World War II Veteran	World War II Veteran
Berkley, Michigan	Eastpointe, Michigan	Macomb, Michigan	Livonia, Michigan	Warren, Michigan
Earl H. Meyers	Gerald R. Pearsall	Charles P. Schaefer	Darvine Strobridge	Floyd F. Yeager
World War II Veteran	World War II Veteran	World War II Veteran	World War II Veteran	World War II Veteran
Southgate, Michigan	Grosse Pointe Woods, Michigan	Beverly Hills, Michigan	Rochester Hills, Michigan	Troy, Michigan
Shirley M. Meyers	Rodney M. Petersen	Philip T. Schmidt	Harold K. Thompson	Francis W. Zidwick
World War II Veteran	World War II Veteran	World War II Veteran	World War II Veteran	World War II Veteran
Southgate, Michigan	Birmingham, Michigan	Livonia, Michigan	Troy, Michigan	Bloomfield Hills, Michigan
Gordon R. Michaelson	James E. Reid	Donald J. Sherman	Harmon Tron	Eugene H. Zylinski
World War II Veteran	World War II Veteran	World War II Veteran	World War II Veteran	World War II Veteran
Grosse Pointe Woods, Michigan	Pontiac, Michigan	Northville, Michigan	Southfield, Michigan	Ypsilanti, Michigan

Honor Flight 7 Saturday, October 13, 2007

More photos of this trip at www.honorflightmichigan.com

Judith L. Berry	Michael G. Ceaser	Rose Karam	Magaret E. Schaefer	Michael D. Withee
Medical Personnel	Trip Guardian	Trip Guardian	Trip Guardian	Trip Guardian
Huntington Woods, Michigan	Riverview, Michigan	Macomb, Michigan	Beverly Hills, Michigan	Troy, Michigan
Marie Doherty	Sharon L. Champine	Catherine C. Keenan	Timothy N. Standfest	William A. Yauch
Medical Personnel	Trip Guardian	Trip Guardian	Trip Guardian	Trip Guardian
Berkley, Michigan	Troy, Michigan	Merrill, Michigan	China, Michigan	Urbana, Illinois
Michael M. Matthews-Penn	Michael Culverhouse	Mary C. Keenan	Edward M. Staniek	
Medical Personnel	Trip Guardian	Trip Guardian	Trip Guardian	
Berkley, Michigan	Lake Orion, Michigan	Urbana, Illinois	Auburn Hills, Michigan	
Linda K. Brack	Melissa A. Downey	Donna L. Lamb	Kathy Stannis	
Trip Guardian	Trip Guardian	Trip Guardian	Trip Guardian	
Royal Oak, Michigan	Huntington Woods, Michigan	Clinton Township, Michigan	Berkley, Michigan	
Sharron A. Byers	Timothy Downey	William E. Leafdale	Ayleet "Bud" Wease	
Trip Guardian	Trip Guardian	Trip Guardian	Trip Guardian	
Grosse Ile, Michigan	Huntington Woods, Michigan	Rochester Hills, Michigan	Royal Oak, Michigan	
Justin R. Cabe	Theadora C. Gansmiller	Catherine F. Matthews-Penn	William P. White	
Trip Guardian	Trip Guardian	Trip Guardian	Trip Guardian	
Clinton Township, Michigan	Jackson, Michigan	Berkley, Michigan	Macomb, Michigan	

Battle of Midway June 4-7, 1942

"They had no right to win. Yet they did, and in doing so they changed the course of a war...even against the greatest of odds, there is something in the human spirit – a magic blend of skill, faith and valor – that can lift men from certain defeat to incredible victory."

– Walter Lord, Author

Mt. Clemens, Michigan   Pontiac, Michigan   Warren, Michigan   St.Clair Shores, Michigan   Westland, Michigan

Richard J. Bell
World War II Veteran
Shelby Township, Michigan

Arthur S. Corry
World War II Veteran
Port Huron, Michigan

Gerald S. Dinser
World War II Veteran
Whitmore Lake, Michigan

Joseph Gaglio
World War II Veteran
St. Clair Shores, Michigan

Jimmy B. Jardack
World War II Veteran
Beverly Hills, Michigan

Raymond G. Black
World War II Veteran
Pontiac, Michigan

Robert W. Coulter
World War II Veteran
Port Huron, Michigan

Michael A. Diviney
World War II Veteran
Ortonville, Michigan

Christ Geoga
World War II Veteran
Clinton Township, Michigan

Peter J. Kernan
World War II Veteran
Grosse Pointe Shores, Michigan

Edward L. Bohde
World War II Veteran
St.Clair Shores, Michigan

Gidio Culos
World War II Veteran
St. Clair Shores, Michigan

Robert L. Dondero
World War II Veteran
Royal Oak, Michigan

Nathaniel A. Gray
World War II Veteran
Warren, Michigan

Creighton Kerr
World War II Veteran
Waterford, Michigan

Harry P. Klenner World War II Veteran Southgate, Michigan	**Denis MacDonald** World War II Veteran Dearborn, Michigan	**John S. Pink** World War II Veteran South Lyon, Michigan	**John G. Searight** World War II Veteran Clarkston, Michigan	**William Thomas** World War II Veteran Royal Oak, Michigan
Joseph P. Kovach World War II Veteran Houghton Lake, Michigan	**William D. MacPhee** World War II Veteran Royal Oak, Michigan	**James E. Pogue** World War II Veteran Farmington, Michigan	**Casimir R. Skalski** World War II Veteran Warren, Michigan	**Sidney Upton** World War II Veteran Royal Oak, Michigan
George R. Krausmann World War II Veteran Clinton Township, Michigan	**Arnold P. Malinchak** World War II Veteran Sterling Heights, Michigan	**Ralph A. Reid** World War II Veteran Waterford, Michigan	**Chester T. Sokolowski** World War II Veteran Southfield, Michigan	**Norris C. Wetters** World War II Veteran Beverly Hills, Michigan
Robert D. Kremer World War II Veteran Royal Oak, Michigan	**Joseph M. Manzella** World War II Veteran Mears, Michigan	**Gerald F. Reidel** World War II Veteran Clinton Township, Michigan	**Michael Soley** World War II Veteran Lenox, Michigan	**Clyde R. Whitledge** World War II Veteran Harrison Township, Michigan
Dorothy F. Lookabaugh World War II Veteran Pontiac, Michigan	**Ronald W. Mason** World War II Veteran Ann Arbor, Michigan	**Lew Rose** World War II Veteran West Bloomfield, Michigan	**Edna M. Somers** World War II Veteran Plymouth, Michigan	**Marvin E. Williams** World War II Veteran Highland, Michigan
Bernard P. Lyons World War II Veteran Fort Gratiot, Michigan	**Robert L. Nagel** World War II Veteran Royal Oak, Michigan	**Gale E. Scafe** World War II Veteran Clarkston, Michigan	**Carl L. Sumner** World War II Veteran Southgate, Michigan	**Duane L. Zemper** World War II Veteran Howell, Michigan
Gerald E. Marsh World War II Veteran Ortonville, Michigan	**James D. Oneill** World War II Veteran Southfield, Michigan	**Jack R. Schram** World War II Veteran Troy, Michigan	**Richard C. Tabaka** World War II Veteran Houghton Lake, Michigan	**Joseph W. Zikewich** World War II Veteran Lake Orion, Michigan
Warren R. Matice World War II Veteran Birmingham, Michigan	**Frank Panley** World War II Veteran Warren, Michigan	**Glenn G. Schuster** World War II Veteran St. Clair Shores, Michigan	**Barry E. Tarbush** World War II Veteran Warren, Michigan	**Robert W. Zuker** World War II Veteran St. Johns, Michigan

Honor Flight 8 — Saturday, November 3, 2007

More photos of this trip at www.honorflightmichigan.com

Diane L. Dengate
Medical Personnel
Ferndale, Michigan

Cynthia L. Canty
Trip Guardian
Birmingham, Michigan

Dianne Jochum
Trip Guardian
Macomb, Michigan

Sheila J. Ricketts
Trip Guardian
Brighton, Michigan

Catherine L. Zimmerman
Trip Guardian
Royal Oak, Michigan

Elizabeth B. Milan
Medical Personnel
Royal Oak, Michigan

Maureen E. Carroll
Trip Guardian
Royal Oak, Michigan

Catherine A. Kavanaugh
Trip Guardian
Dearborn, Michigan

Mark D. Stutzmann
Trip Guardian
Ann Arbor, Michigan

Ethel M. Putala
Medical Personnel
Plymouth, Michigan

Donald R. Chisholm
Trip Guardian
Royal Oak, Michigan

Harry P. Klenner
Trip Guardian
Westland, Michigan

Dennis C. Sumner
Trip Guardian
Canton, Michigan

Chris Zimmel
Medical Personnel
Clawson, Michigan

Carol S. Coden
Trip Guardian
Bloomfield Hills, Michigan

Mary D. Kovach
Trip Guardian
Milford, Michigan

Kevin J. Sutherland
Trip Guardian
Royal Oak, Michigan

Brad P. Ziegler
Official Photographer
West Bloomfield, Michigan

Joyce L. Fisher
Trip Guardian
Howell, Michigan

Russell Levine
Trip Guardian
Huntington Woods, Michigan

William J. Thomas
Trip Guardian
Royal Oak, Michigan

Nancy S. Abentrod
Trip Guardian
Birmingham, Michigan

Dorothy J. Gresnick
Trip Guardian
Beverly Hills, Michigan

Peg M. Moore
Trip Guardian
Ann Arbor, Michigan

Ayleet "Bud" Wease
Trip Guardian
Royal Oak, Michigan

D-Day June 6, 1944

" You are about to embark upon the great crusade toward which we have striven these many months. The eyes of the world are upon you…I have full confidence in your courage, devotion to duty and skill in battle. "

– General Dwight D. Eisenhower

Walter W. Brown
World War II Veteran
Oxford, Michigan

William H. Hansen
World War II Veteran
Grosse Pointe, Michigan

Richard W. Mathew
World War II Veteran
Rochester Hills, Michigan

Richard J. O'Donohue
World War II Veteran
Novi, Michigan

Donald D. Wagner
World War II Veteran
Warren, Michigan

Sam Caldarea
World War II Veteran
Dearborn, Michigan

William F. Heyde
World War II Veteran
Grosse Pointe Woods, Michigan

John McAllister
World War II Veteran
Farmington Hills, Michigan

Steve A. Preston
World War II Veteran
Shelby Township, Michigan

Howard R. Webb
World War II Veteran
Sylvan Lake, Michigan

John Z. Campian
World War II Veteran
Northville, Michigan

Arthur J. Johnson
World War II Veteran
Grosse Pointe Woods, Michigan

Martin F. McNamara
World War II Veteran
Eaton Rapids, Michigan

Robert E. Ralph
World War II Veteran
Shelby Township, Michigan

Bert Wilmot
World War II Veteran
Novi, Michigan

William B. Compton
World War II Veteran
Walled Lake, Michigan

Arthur A. Kaczmarek
World War II Veteran
Beverly Hills, Michigan

George P. Mellios
World War II Veteran
Shelby Township, Michigan

Bernhardt H. Rust
World War II Veteran
St. Clair Shores, Michigan

Joseph J. Zimmel
World War II Veteran
Royal Oak, Michigan

James E. Delaney
World War II Veteran
Lake Orion, Michigan

Michael P. Keith
World War II Veteran
Waterford, Michigan

Harry R. Mitchell
World War II Veteran
Bloomfield Hills, Michigan

Harry Sado
World War II Veteran
Troy, Michigan

————

John F. Dolot
World War II Veteran
Warren, Michigan

Harold C. Kesner
World War II Veteran
Grosse Pointe Woods, Michigan

Traian Moga
World War II Veteran
Canton, Michigan

Raymond F. Saganski
World War II Veteran
Sterling Heights, Michigan

Richard P. Sage
Trip Leader
Royal Oak, Michigan

Mark R. Ennes
World War II Veteran
Sterling Heights, Michigan

Edward L. Knighton
World War II Veteran
South Lyon, Michigan

Malcolm Muszynski
World War II Veteran
River Rouge, Michigan

Earl Stan
World War II Veteran
Southgate, Michigan

Susan Berg
Medical Personnel
Grosse Pointe Woods, Michigan

Philip G. Gerlach
World War II Veteran
Grosse Pointe Shores, Michigan

Armand W. Knorr
World War II Veteran
Eastpointe, Michigan

Melvin Muszynski
World War II Veteran
Southgate, Michigan

Sherwin Vine
World War II Veteran
Birmingham, Michigan

Chris Zimmel
Medical Personnel
Clawson, Michigan

Brad P. Ziegler
Official Photographer
West Bloomfield, Michigan

David A. Kesner
Trip Guardian
Grosse Pointe Woods, Michigan

Richard J. Birchmeier
Trip Guardian
Auburn Hills, Michigan

Beverly A. Kimbro
Trip Guardian
Farmington Hills, Michigan

Robert W. Boucher
Trip Guardian
Canton, Michigan

Gary L. Nicks
Trip Guardian
Rochester Hills, Michigan

Edward Burkhardt
Trip Guardian
Royal Oak, Michigan

Brenda Piekarski
Trip Guardian
Chesterfield, Michigan

Donna M. Duberg
Trip Guardian
St. Louis, Missouri

Anne G. Stoehr
Trip Guardian
Grosse Pointe Woods, Michigan

Mary T. Fullan
Trip Guardian
West Bloomfield, Michigan

John R. Vance
Trip Guardian
Big Rapids, Michigan

Joyce L. Hazelroth
Trip Guardian
Shelby Township, Michigan

Ayleet "Bud" Wease
Trip Guardian
Royal Oak, Michigan

Susan K. Johnson
Trip Guardian
Oxford, Michigan

Catherine L. Zimmerman
Trip Guardian
Royal Oak, Michigan

"THANK YOU for the trip to Washington, D.C. My brother Carl and I were very appreciative of the honor. It was, indeed, a trip never to be forgotten, and on which we could never have afforded on our own."

– Proud World War II Veteran
Honor Flight Michigan Alumnus

Honor Flight 9 Saturday, April 19, 2008
More photos of this trip at www.honorflightmichigan.com

Kermit E. Beverly
World War II Veteran
St. Clair Shores, Michigan

Lawrence H. De Young
World War II Veteran
Beverly Hills, Michigan

Gordon O. Klein
World War II Veteran
Dearborn Heights, Michigan

Herbert H. Rosenberg
World War II Veteran
Southfield, Michigan

William H. Thompson
World War II Veteran
Detroit, Michigan

Wesley R. Blohm
World War II Veteran
Saginaw, Michigan

Tony T. Di Marco
World War II Veteran
Taylor, Michigan

Charles R. Lowry
World War II Veteran
Taylor, Michigan

Felix A. Rotter
World War II Veteran
Plymouth, Michigan

Everett A. Trudell
World War II Veteran
Milford, Michigan

John J. Bruneel
World War II Veteran
Harper Woods, Michigan

Donald R. Elgas
World War II Veteran
Prudenville, Michigan

George Lusko
World War II Veteran
Dearborn Heights, Michigan

Richard E. Rutz
World War II Veteran
Waterford, Michigan

Merrill Valentine
World War II Veteran
Livonia, Michigan

Frederik E. Bush
World War II Veteran
Farmington Hills, Michigan

Sheldon Feuer
World War II Veteran
Shelby Township, Michigan

John W. Marker
World War II Veteran
Livonia, Michigan

Walter W. Schave
World War II Veteran
St. Clair Shores, Michigan

Louis L. Vickovic
World War II Veteran
Warren, Michigan

Edward P. Cebulski
World War II Veteran
Dearborn, Michigan

Raymond W. Frank
World War II Veteran
St. Clair Shores, Michigan

Robert V. McCabe
World War II Veteran
Novi, Michigan

Max H. Schrader
World War II Veteran
Traverse City, Michigan

Donald L. Weatherup
World War II Veteran
St. Clair Shores, Michigan

Norman C. Cook
World War II Veteran
West Branch, Michigan

Margarito Garcia
World War II Veteran
Rochester, Michigan

James M. McDonald
World War II Veteran
Farmington Hills, Michigan

Patrick R. Stewart
World War II Veteran
Inkster, Michigan

Robert E. Whitlow
World War II Veteran
Waterford, Michigan

Betty J. Crosby
World War II Veteran
Rochester Hills, Michigan

Mario Gizzi
World War II Veteran
Allen Park, Michigan

Edgar A. Millner
World War II Veteran
Shelby Township, Michigan

Leonard J. Stockoski
World War II Veteran
Royal Oak, Michigan

Theodore R. Widgren
World War II Veteran
Royal Oak, Michigan

Frank V. Curry
World War II Veteran
Canton, Michigan

David G. Guindon
World War II Veteran
Warren, Michigan

Warren A. Ottinger
World War II Veteran
Allen Park, Michigan

Raymond R. Suarez
World War II Veteran
Redford, Michigan

Gerald E. Zubalik
World War II Veteran
Waterford, Michigan

Jack L. Hegwood
Trip Guardian
Clinton Township, Michigan

Richard P. Sage
Trip Leader
Royal Oak, Michigan

Diane M. Hoover
Trip Guardian
Royal Oak, Michigan

Cynthia F. McKenna
Medical Personnel
Rochester Hills, Michigan

Nancy C. Klein
Trip Guardian
Livonia, Michigan

Brad P. Ziegler
Official Photographer
West Bloomfield, Michigan

Kathy A. Krause
Trip Guardian
Shelby Township, Michigan

Edward Burkhardt
Trip Guardian
Royal Oak, Michigan

Michael A. McCabe
Trip Guardian
Wixom, Michigan

Sybil M. De Young
Trip Guardian
Beverly Hills, Michigan

Theodore H. Quisenberry
Trip Guardian
Royal Oak, Michigan

David J. Dunaj
Trip Guardian
Berkley, Michigan

Kevin J. Sutherland
Trip Guardian
Royal Oak, Michigan

Sharon Good
Trip Guardian
West Bloomfield, Michigan

Ayleet "Bud" Wease
Trip Guardian
Royal Oak, Michigan

"The heroism of our own troops...was matched by that of the armed forces of the nations that fought by our side...they absorbed the blows... and they shared to the full in the ultimate destruction of the enemy."

– President Harry S. Truman

Honor Flight 10
Saturday, May 3, 2008
More photos of this trip at www.honorflightmichigan.com

Donald A. Arnett World War II Veteran Novi, Michigan	**Richard L. Crawley** World War II Veteran Commerce Township, Michigan	**Markus Kelly** World War II Veteran Inkster, Michigan	**Leonard F. Parent** World War II Veteran Chesterfield, Michigan	**Albert Sundell** World War II Veteran Temperance, Michigan
James N. Bird World War II Veteran Birmingham, Michigan	**Dorothy M. Davis** World War II Veteran Pontiac, Michigan	**Raymond F. Kosciolek** World War II Veteran Algonac, Michigan	**Betty A. Peterson** World War II Veteran Oak Park, Michigan	**Kenneth E. Thorburn** World War II Veteran Davison, Michigan
Richard A. Blavatt World War II Veteran Madison Heights, Michigan	**John L. DeNardo** World War II Veteran Clinton Township, Michigan	**John Lazo** World War II Veteran Pinckney, Michigan	**Elizabeth A. Potter** World War II Veteran Rochester Hills, Michigan	**William Troy** World War II Veteran Redford, Michigan
Ralph C. Bolz World War II Veteran Livonia, Michigan	**Herbert P. Eidelman** World War II Veteran West Bloomfield, Michigan	**Charles R. Markham** World War II Veteran Brighton, Michigan	**Keith J. Potter** World War II Veteran Rochester Hills, Michigan	**David Wakefield** World War II Veteran Kalamazoo, Michigan
William D. Brown World War II Veteran Westland, Michigan	**Leonard M. Fandale** World War II Veteran Troy, Michigan	**Nicholas Mihut** World War II Veteran Madison Heights, Michigan	**John S. Reiff** World War II Veteran Northville, Michigan	**John S. Wilson** World War II Veteran Haslett, Michigan
Robert G. Brunner World War II Veteran Shelby Township, Michigan	**Robert E. Gesquiere** World War II Veteran Bay City, Michigan	**Plezzy L. Newingham** World War II Veteran Waterford, Michigan	**Jack G. Rickerman** World War II Veteran Clawson, Michigan	**Roman J. Zedro** World War II Veteran Utica, Michigan

11

Richard P. Sage
Trip Leader
Royal Oak, Michigan

Cheryl A. Thorburn
Medical Personnel
Flint, Michigan

Chris Zimmel
Medical Personnel
Clawson, Michigan

Elizabeth A. Antilla
Trip Guardian
Port Huron, Michigan

Becky J. Chadwick
Trip Guardian
Trenton, Michigan

Mark A. Fandale
Trip Guardian
Oak Park, Michigan

Charles S. Johnson
Trip Guardian
White Lake, Michigan

Carol Kavanaugh-Burgess
Trip Guardian
Warren, Michigan

Catherine A. Kavanaugh
Press - Media
Dearborn, Michigan

Richard M. Price
Trip Guardian
Brighton, Michigan

Virginia R. Reiff
Trip Guardian
Northville, Michigan

Pamela M. Robbins
Trip Guardian
Royal Oak, Michigan

Kim E. Stafford
Trip Guardian
Dearborn, Michigan

Norman P. VanSparrentak
Trip Guardian
Sterling Heights, Michigan

Anne L. Walts
Trip Guardian
Commerce Township, Michigan

" Each man must for himself alone decide what is right and what is wrong, which course is patriotic and which isn't. "

– Mark Twain, American Writer

Honor Flight 11 Saturday, May 17, 2008

More photos of this trip at www.honorflightmichigan.com

Robert F. Bergy	Anton A. Danek	Morris L. Kapplinger	Raymond A. Parzych	Howard J. Steffes
World War II Veteran	World War II Veteran	World War II Veteran	World War II Veteran	World War II Veteran
Clare, Michigan	Owosso, Michigan	Farwell, Michigan	Northville, Michigan	Troy, Michigan
John E. Booth	William J. Evans	Earl R. Kidder	Clemens Pruski	John H. Strock
World War II Veteran	World War II Veteran	World War II Veteran	World War II Veteran	World War II Veteran
Walled Lake, Michigan	Troy, Michigan	Northville, Michigan	Warren, Michigan	Waterford, Michigan
Gene L. Brandon	Arthur P. Fayroian	William B. Kindred	Miguel M. Quezada	Louis R. VanCuyl
World War II Veteran	World War II Veteran	World War II Veteran	World War II Veteran	World War II Veteran
Clare, Michigan	Royal Oak, Michigan	Allen Park, Michigan	Southfield, Michigan	Howell, Michigan
Daniel S. Brant	James R. Flannigan	Henry E. Largin	Ralph H. Raeder	James A. Viers
World War II Veteran	World War II Veteran	World War II Veteran	World War II Veteran	World War II Veteran
Warren, Michigan	Allen Park, Michigan	Morley, Michigan	Lincoln Park, Michigan	Westland, Michigan
Roman Broda	Milton George	David J. Levy	Richard F. Runyan	Ellis K. Zink
World War II Veteran	World War II Veteran	World War II Veteran	World War II Veteran	World War II Veteran
Dearborn, Michigan	Dearborn, Michigan	Southfield, Michigan	Sturgis, Michigan	Rochester Hills, Michigan
Gerald E. Burde	Willard A. Gieske	Jack Levy	Joseph F. Sanfilippo	
World War II Veteran	World War II Veteran	World War II Veteran	World War II Veteran	
Fort Gratiot, Michigan	Harrison, Michigan	Beverly Hills, Michigan	Allen Park, Michigan	

12

Ayleet "Bud" Wease
Trip Leader
Royal Oak, Michigan

Kevin M. Kosal
Medical Personnel
Wolverine Lake, Michigan

Brad P. Ziegler
Official Photographer
West Bloomfield, Michigan

Billy M. Apostolopoulos
Trip Guardian
Belleville, Michigan

Thomas C. Brant
Trip Guardian
Troy, Michigan

Edward Burkhardt
Trip Guardian
Royal Oak, Michigan

Nancy A. Calvert
Trip Guardian
Warren, Michigan

Thomas A. Danek
Trip Guardian
Canton, Michigan

Curtis L. Foreman
Trip Guardian
Oak Park, Michigan

William P. George
Trip Guardian
Canton, Michigan

Richard J. Levy
Trip Guardian
Royal Oak, Michigan

Charles J. Peltier
Trip Guardian
South Lyon, Michigan

Catherine L. Zimmerman
Trip Guardian
Royal Oak, Michigan

Kenneth E. Zink
Trip Guardian
Troy, Michigan

" The visits to the World War II Memorial
and the Arlington National Cemetery
were emotionally beyond belief. This self-
professed cynical and thick-skinned old guy
was intensely moved by these beautiful and
thought-provoking sites. "

– Proud World War II Veteran
Honor Flight Michigan Alumnus

Honor Flight 12 Saturday, June 7, 2008

More photos of this trip at www.honorflightmichigan.com

Robert K. Anderson	Roy H. Hoke	Edward A. Mroczek	Bernard W. Schihl	Debra A. Shipman
World War II Veteran	World War II Veteran	World War II Veteran	World War II Veteran	Medical Personnel
Sand Point, Michigan	West Bloomfield, Michigan	Sandusky, Michigan	Farmington Hills, Michigan	Oxford, Michigan
Bernard H. Brehm	Charles D. Kalman	Marvin E. Muehl	William R. Semperger	Deanna L. Tucker
World War II Veteran	World War II Veteran	World War II Veteran	World War II Veteran	Medical Personnel
Plymouth, Michigan	Flat Rock, Michigan	Clinton Township, Michigan	Clarkston, Michigan	Lake Orion, Michigan
Paul J. Coapman	George V. Lietzau	Donald R. Nadeau	Frazer M. Swanger	Nate Strong
World War II Veteran	World War II Veteran	World War II Veteran	World War II Veteran	Official Photographer
Shelby Township, Michigan	Novi, Michigan	Stanwood, Michigan	Dearborn, Michigan	Wixom, Michigan
Stephen A. Cole	Raymond W. Lumley	Ray A. Pine	George C. Thompson	Marion T. Coapman
World War II Veteran	World War II Veteran	World War II Veteran	World War II Veteran	Trip Guardian
Rochester, Michigan	Livonia, Michigan	Redford, Michigan	Clarkston, Michigan	Shelby Township, Michigan
John M. Hanson	Floyd C. Martlock	Carter E. Porter	Allen R. Young	Nancy E. Cutsinger
World War II Veteran	World War II Veteran	World War II Veteran	World War II Veteran	Trip Guardian
Bloomfield Hills, Michigan	Berkley, Michigan	Plymouth, Michigan	Plymouth, Michigan	West Bloomfield, Michigan
Carl W. Heinowski	Louis Martlock	Keith A. Poulson		Kelly J. Domigan
World War II Veteran	World War II Veteran	World War II Veteran		Trip Guardian
Hillsdale, Michigan	Rochester Hills, Michigan	Oxford, Michigan		Woodhaven, Michigan

13

Louise C. Downs
Trip Guardian
Metamora, Michigan

Kathy M. Hoke
Trip Guardian
Waterford, Michigan

Stephanie L. Hyska
Trip Guardian
Clinton Township, Michigan

Darlene Johnson
Trip Guardian
Dryden, Michigan

Linda J. Klais
Trip Guardian
Howell, Michigan

John K. Kroll
Trip Guardian
Southgate, Michigan

James J. Lapham
Trip Guardian
Commerce Township, Michigan

John E. Lapham
Trip Guardian
Novi, Michigan

Julie A. LaRocque
Trip Guardian
Westland, Michigan

Mark A. Lumley
Trip Guardian
Novi, Michigan

Carol A. Margiotta
Trip Guardian
Commerce, Michigan

Delores A. Martin
Trip Guardian
Waterford, Michigan

Michael D. McCarthy
Trip Guardian
Southfield, Michigan

Veronica J. Pinto
Trip Guardian
Trenton, Michigan

David K. Poulson
Trip Guardian
DeWitt, Michigan

Marcia K. Rogers
Trip Guardian
Warren, Michigan

Patrick M. Valentine
Trip Guardian
Gibraltar, Michigan

"December 7, 1941, a date which will live in infamy... no matter how long it may take us to overcome this premeditated invasion, the American people, in their righteous might, will win through to absolute victory."

– President Franklin D. Roosevelt

Honor Flight 13 Saturday, June 21, 2008

More photos of this trip at www.honorflightmichigan.com

Arthur D. Anderson
World War II Veteran
Northville, Michigan

Benjamin H. Clary
World War II Veteran
Shelby Township, Michigan

George T. Holsworth
World War II Veteran
Clarkston, Michigan

Ervin Manson
World War II Veteran
West Bloomfield, Michigan

Salvatore M. Scozzari
World War II Veteran
Farwell, Michigan

Joseph H. Arens
World War II Veteran
Capac, Michigan

Howard L. DeKarsky
World War II Veteran
Dearborn, Michigan

Norman R. Hughes
World War II Veteran
Rochester Hills, Michigan

Ivan D. McPherson
World War II Veteran
Millington, Michigan

Bernard L. Shellman
World War II Veteran
Brownstown, Michigan

Leo V. Arens
World War II Veteran
Harrison Township, Michigan

Marvin H. Duckett
World War II Veteran
Farmington Hills, Michigan

Harold J. Humphreys
World War II Veteran
Clinton Township, Michigan

John P. Mulherin
World War II Veteran
Rockwood, Michigan

Robert J. Smith
World War II Veteran
Canton, Michigan

Leo A. Barris
World War II Veteran
Walled Lake, Michigan

Stacy L. Elliott
World War II Veteran
Clinton Township, Michigan

Lovell J. Jackson
World War II Veteran
Detroit, Michigan

Richard R. Nowicke
World War II Veteran
Allen Park, Michigan

William E. Smyth
World War II Veteran
Wixom, Michigan

Arthur R. Blezenski
World War II Veteran
Chesterfield, Michigan

Glenn A. Erickson
World War II Veteran
Muskegon, Michigan

Nicholas X. Karay
World War II Veteran
Temperance, Michigan

Charles W. Pannell
World War II Veteran
Fenton, Michigan

Robert A. Stone
World War II Veteran
Novi, Michigan

Dale V. Boker
World War II Veteran
Royal Oak, Michigan

Carl D. Gaerig
World War II Veteran
Dearborn, Michigan

Frederick W. Kingston
World War II Veteran
Plymouth, Michigan

Joseph Piersante
World War II Veteran
Clinton Township, Michigan

Rolland Walt
World War II Veteran
Farmington Hills, Michigan

Wilbur J. Breault
World War II Veteran
South Lyon, Michigan

Ruth G. Gaerig
World War II Veteran
Dearborn, Michigan

Keith W. Lemmon
World War II Veteran
Dearborn, Michigan

Herman Preston
World War II Veteran
Pontiac, Michigan

Robert F. Zang
World War II Veteran
Commerce Township, Michigan

Donald M. Carlson
World War II Veteran
Clinton Township, Michigan

Irving Gladstone
World War II Veteran
Livonia, Michigan

Edward W. Lewandowski
World War II Veteran
Farmington, Michigan

Marvin J. Salzwedel
World War II Veteran
Westland, Michigan

William Zucker
World War II Veteran
West Bloomfield, Michigan

Shirley A. Moore
Trip Guardian
Commerce Township, Michigan

Richard P. Sage
Trip Leader
Royal Oak, Michigan

Robert C. Niskar
Trip Guardian
Farmington Hills, Michigan

Lois A. Hancock
Medical Personnel
Novi, Michigan

Beverly J. Shaw
Trip Guardian
Clarkston, Michigan

Nate Strong
Official Photographer
Wixom, Michigan

Kevin Sutherland
Trip Guardian
Royal Oak, Michigan

Donovan M. Abram
Trip Guardian
Sterling Heights, Michigan

Sean P. Tracy
Trip Guardian
Wixom, Michigan

Edward Burkhardt
Trip Guardian
Royal Oak, Michigan

David L. Wayne
Trip Guardian
Canton, Michigan

Ronald D. Horvath
Trip Guardian
Ypsilanti, Michigan

William D. Welch
Trip Guardian
Royal Oak, Michigan

Greg J. Keys
Trip Guardian
Royal Oak, Michigan

Katherine A. Williams
Trip Guardian
Lansing, Michigan

"I will be forever grateful for the wonderful opportunity to participate in the Michigan Honor Flight. Thank you for the heartfelt kindness and generosity. Last but not least to all the helpful guardians."

– Proud World War II Veteran
Honor Flight Michigan Alumnus

Honor Flight 14 Saturday, July 12, 2008

More photos of this trip at www.honorflightmichigan.com

Manfred Galdes World War II Veteran Roscommon, Michigan	**Robert W. Kahle** World War II Veteran Metamora, Michigan	**Glen B. McCurdy** World War II Veteran Detroit, Michigan	**Richard V. Quinn** World War II Veteran Kalamazoo, Michigan	**Leonard A. Shaffer** World War II Veteran Metamora, Michigan
Theodore J. Gancos World War II Veteran Livonia, Michigan	**Ora N. Keys** World War II Veteran Fenton, Michigan	**Thomas M. Meagher** World War II Veteran St. Clair Shores, Michigan	**Fred H. Rahn** World War II Veteran Warren, Michigan	**Francis V. Stanco** World War II Veteran Detroit, Michigan
Henry J. Gosztyla World War II Veteran Warren, Michigan	**William A. King** World War II Veteran Royal Oak, Michigan	**Clemens R. Misiak** World War II Veteran Melvin, Michigan	**James L. Rickets** World War II Veteran Westland, Michigan	**Roy Stricker** World War II Veteran Rogers City, Michigan
Ethel S. Grossman World War II Veteran Southfield, Michigan	**Julius Kucab** World War II Veteran Rochester Hills, Michigan	**Alfred J. Morad** World War II Veteran Northville, Michigan	**Francis Rogers** World War II Veteran Westland, Michigan	**Thomas L. Tomlinson** World War II Veteran St. Clair Shores, Michigan
Calvin W. Hanawalt World War II Veteran Redford, Michigan	**Melvin J. LaFave** World War II Veteran Clinton Township, Michigan	**Theodore L. Mullett** World War II Veteran Dearborn, Michigan	**Harvey J. Rowland** World War II Veteran Grayling, Michigan	**Phyllis B. Trestler** World War II Veteran Northville, Michigan
William B. Hanford World War II Veteran Howell, Michigan	**John Laing** World War II Veteran Rochester Hills, Michigan	**Doyle Nye** World War II Veteran Lake City, Michigan	**Antone Santos** World War II Veteran Mount Clemens, Michigan	**Thomas E. Trestler** World War II Veteran Northville, Michigan

Pamela M. Robbins
Trip Leader
Royal Oak, Michigan

Christine Zimmel
Medical Personnel
Clawson, Michigan

Brad P. Ziegler
Official Photographer
West Bloomfield, Michigan

Ryan Burgess
Trip Guardian
Warren, Michigan

Lowell A. Johnson
Trip Guardian
Clarkston, Michigan

Carol Kavanaugh-Burgess
Trip Guardian
Warren, Michigan

Robert D. Lenger
Trip Guardian
Holland, Michigan

Donald F. Maatz
Trip Guardian
Grosse Ile., Michigan

Michael P. Metz
Trip Guardian
Troy, Michigan

Gary L. Mooneyham
Trip Guardian
Clarkston, Michigan

Wanda M. Nelson
Trip Guardian
Davison, Michigan

Bruce L. Pharis
Trip Guardian
Royal Oak, Michigan

Vicki Selva
Trip Guardian
Macomb, Michigan

Ayleet "Bud" Wease
Trip Guardian
Royal Oak, Michigan

Douglas J. Wiles
Trip Guardian
Powell, Ohio

"Wars may be fought with weapons, but they are won by men. It is the spirit of men who follow and of the man who leads that gains the victory."

– General George S. Patton

Honor Flight 15 Saturday, July 26, 2008
More photos of this trip at www.honorflightmichigan.com

Russell A. Ash World War II Veteran Plymouth, Michigan	**Louis Caponi** World War II Veteran Madison Heights, Michigan	**William A. Irwin** World War II Veteran Vassar, Michigan	**John R. Novasky** World War II Veteran Westland, Michigan	**Daniel G. Taggart** World War II Veteran Beverly Hills, Michigan
Marvel H. Bakke World War II Veteran Harper Woods, Michigan	**Louis W. Delp** World War II Veteran Tavaros, Florida	**Franklin E. Kveen** World War II Veteran Northville, Michigan	**Arden C. Olmstead** World War II Veteran Royal Oak, Michigan	**Russel A. White** World War II Veteran Metamora, Michigan
James K. Barnes World War II Veteran White Lake, Michigan	**Lincoln Dodd** World War II Veteran Spring Lake, Michigan	**George K. Lewis** World War II Veteran Northville, Michigan	**Frank J. Osebold** World War II Veteran Clinton Township, Michigan	**Leroy C. Witter** World War II Veteran Pinckney, Michigan
Lester W. Bell World War II Veteran Dearborn, Michigan	**Benjamin E. Ewing** World War II Veteran Bloomfield Hills, Michigan	**Melvin Marsch** World War II Veteran Livonia, Michigan	**George P. Page** World War II Veteran Woodhaven, Michigan	**Roy E. Wolf** World War II Veteran Westland, Michigan
Woodrow W. Berryhill World War II Veteran Livonia, Michigan	**Donald D. Falk** World War II Veteran Clark Lake, Michigan	**Raymond C. Mihelcic** World War II Veteran West Bloomfield, Michigan	**Clayton D. Penzien** World War II Veteran Centerline, Michigan	**Andrew Wong** World War II Veteran Beverly Hills, Michigan
Dagmar M. Brown World War II Veteran Cass City, Michigan	**Eugene Glime** World War II Veteran Troy, Michigan	**Donald G. Molloy** World War II Veteran Sterling Heights, Michigan	**Alfred W. Pobocik** World War II Veteran Midland, Michigan	

Ayleet "Bud" Wease
Trip Leader
Royal Oak, Michigan

Leanne L. Davenport
Medical Personnel
West Bloomfield, Michigan

Barbara J. Solms
Medical Personnel
Royal Oak, Michigan

Luther B. Anderson
Trip Guardian
Rochester Hills, Michigan

Dennis V. Andrzejak
Trip Guardian
Royal Oak, Michigan

David J. Caponi
Trip Guardian
Lake Orion, Michigan

Joyce T. Carbaugh
Trip Guardian
Kaplan, Louisiana

Sheryl L. Daniloff
Trip Guardian
Clinton Township, Michigan

Diane M. Hamilton
Trip Guardian
Eastpointe, Michigan

Alan S. Herccg
Trip Guardian
Holt, Michigan

Kathy Lochmann
Trip Guardian
Plymouth, Michigan

William C. Rossow
Trip Guardian
Northville, Michigan

Linda A. Russell
Trip Guardian
Clinton Township, Michigan

Barbara J. Wickham
Trip Guardian
Clinton Township, Michigan

Catherine L. Zimmerman
Trip Guardian
Royal Oak, Michigan

"I had the privilege of an Honor Flight a few weeks ago. I would like to thank you all for a most wonderful day, one I will never forget. I have been around the world but that day tops them all."

– Proud World War II Veteran
Honor Flight Michigan Alumnus

Honor Flight 16 Saturday, August 2, 2008

More photos of this trip at www.honorflightmichigan.com

Noah T. Baxter
World War II Veteran
Northville, Michigan

John Chimko
World War II Veteran
Novi, Michigan

George J. Fulkerson
World War II Veteran
Novi, Michigan

Arthur J. Loesser
World War II Veteran
Troy, Michigan

Ralph J. Rays
World War II Veteran
Novi, Michigan

Edward J. Bayus
World War II Veteran
Novi, Michigan

Henry J. Dehanke
World War II Veteran
Howell, Michigan

Michael Glagola
World War II Veteran
Novi, Michigan

George T. Moy
World War II Veteran
Novi, Michigan

Wilfrid Robinson
World War II Veteran
Novi, Michigan

Ruben Bjerkness
World War II Veteran
Novi, Michigan

David P. Daily
World War II Veteran
Southgate, Michigan

Kenneth D. Hains
World War II Veteran
Novi, Michigan

Jack W. Nice
World War II Veteran
Waterford, Michigan

Robert O. Russman
World War II Veteran
Commerce Township, Michigan

Donald C. Boyd
World War II Veteran
Novi, Michigan

Daniel DeGrave
World War II Veteran
Novi, Michigan

Kenneth C. Hamister
World War II Veteran
Novi, Michigan

Donald G. Olsen
World War II Veteran
Brooklyn, Michigan

Alice C. Smith
World War II Veteran
Novi, Michigan

Harold F. Bradshaw
World War II Veteran
Novi, Michigan

Harry Dornbos
World War II Veteran
Holland, Michigan

Patricia J. Hamister
World War II Veteran
Novi, Michigan

Edward Papelian
World War II Veteran
Novi, Michigan

David Stofer
World War II Veteran
Novi, Michigan

Ernest F. Bulgarelli
World War II Veteran
Novi, Michigan

Willard L. Dresser
World War II Veteran
Novi, Michigan

Oscar Hovsepian
World War II Veteran
Dearborn Heights, Michigan

James M. Payne
World War II Veteran
Novi, Michigan

Richard I. Terpstra
World War II Veteran
Baldwin, Michigan

George H. Butcher
World War II Veteran
Novi, Michigan

Emmanuel G. Felice
World War II Veteran
Troy, Michigan

Harry Kurtjian
World War II Veteran
Allen Park, Michigan

Eugene F. Peters
World War II Veteran
Novi, Michigan

Thomas L. Terry
World War II Veteran
Novi, Michigan

William L. Caryl
World War II Veteran
Novi, Michigan

Stephen Fox
World War II Veteran
Novi, Michigan

Jac LeGoff
World War II Veteran
Novi, Michigan

Manuel M. Pompa
World War II Veteran
Novi, Michigan

Dean F. Wheeler
World War II Veteran
Novi, Michigan

Ayleet "Bud" Wease
Trip Leader
Royal Oak, Michigan

Michelle L. Cassabon
Medical Personnel
Eastpointe, Michigan

Barbara A. Samson
Medical Personnel
White Lake, Michigan

Brad P. Ziegler
Official Photographer
West Bloomfield, Michigan

Edward Burkhardt
Trip Guardian
Royal Oak, Michigan

Douglas P. Burley
Trip Guardian
Pinckney, Michigan

Barbara A. Chirio
Trip Guardian
Novi, Michigan

Keith A. Goulait
Trip Guardian
Ortonville, Michigan

Patrick T. Grady
Trip Guardian
Troy, Michigan

Sharon M. Hunt
Trip Guardian
Waterford, Michigan

John Jasionowicz
Trip Guardian
Rochester Hills, Michigan

Russell L. Knopp
Trip Guardian
Traverse City, Michigan

Julie M. Soyer
Trip Guardian
Ypsilanti, Michigan

Kevin Sutherland
Trip Guardian
Royal Oak, Michigan

Randy R. Talbot
Trip Guardian
Chesterfield, Michigan

"Sure, we want to go home. We want this war over with. The quickest way to get it over with is to go get the bastards who started it."

– General George S. Patton

Honor Flight 17 Saturday, October 4, 2008
More photos of this trip at www.honorflightmichigan.com

086

Mabel V. Carson	Clifford G. Flegel	Lester Kaper	George A. Miller	Donald G. Speyer
World War II Veteran	World War II Veteran	World War II Veteran	World War II Veteran	World War II Veteran
Dearborn, Michigan	Ithaca, Michigan	Holland, Michigan	Dearborn, Michigan	Bloomfield Hills, Michigan
Henry Clark	Donald L. Flegel	William G. Klein	Leo G. Mucha	Stephen Stashuk
World War II Veteran	World War II Veteran	World War II Veteran	World War II Veteran	World War II Veteran
Kentwood, Michigan	Brant, Michigan	Northville, Michigan	Otisville, Michigan	Grosse Pointe Woods, Michigan
Richard L. Confer	Louis D. Giannotta	Roy F. Knudsen	John M. Noraian	Joseph M. Tarchalski
World War II Veteran	World War II Veteran	World War II Veteran	World War II Veteran	World War II Veteran
Northville, Michigan	Warren, Michigan	Rochester Hills, Michigan	Bloomfield Hills, Michigan	Waterford, Michigan
John A. Cooper	Russell L. Halbrook	Fred S. Lee	Harold P. Porter	Henry J. Thomey
World War II Veteran	World War II Veteran	World War II Veteran	World War II Veteran	World War II Veteran
St. Clair Shores, Michigan	Bloomfield Township, Michigan	Farmington Hills, Michigan	Romeo, Michigan	Mio, Michigan
Harry Dakesian	James L. Hawks	Joseph A. Lenart	Leonard W. Schim	Albert N. Vartanian
World War II Veteran	World War II Veteran	World War II Veteran	World War II Veteran	World War II Veteran
West Bloomfield, Michigan	Pentwater, Michigan	Romulus, Michigan	Grosse Pointe Woods, Michigan	Southfield, Michigan
Ray A. Davidson	William R. Hayes	Robert S. Locher	Dudley F. Scott	Richard G. Wilson
World War II Veteran	World War II Veteran	World War II Veteran	World War II Veteran	World War II Veteran
Kentwood, Michigan	Bloomfield Hills, Michigan	Dearborn Heights, Michigan	Howell, Michigan	Jackson, Michigan

Richard P. Sage
Trip Leader
Royal Oak, Michigan

Ann S. McDonald
Medical Personnel
West Bloomfield, Michigan

Nate Strong
Official Photographer
Wixom, Michigan

Joshua P. Famie
Press - Media
Wixom, Michigan

Keith M. Famie
Press - Media
Wixom, Michigan

Christian Kassel
Press - Media
Wixom, Michigan

Joan K. Connell
Trip Guardian
Northville, Michigan

Phillip G. Flegel
Trip Guardian
Elsie, Michigan

Carol Kavanaugh-Burgess
Trip Guardian
Warren, Michigan

Paul M. Locher
Trip Guardian
Ferndale, Michigan

Benjamin C. Logan
Trip Guardian
Wixom, Michigan

James H. McMullen
Trip Guardian
Plymouth, Michigan

Rodney P. Porter
Trip Guardian
Romeo, Michigan

Charles Roeske
Trip Guardian
Dearborn, Michigan

Maureen E. Sage
Trip Guardian
Royal Oak, Michigan

Alan L. Simpson
Trip Guardian
Perry, Michigan

Ronald M. Thomey
Trip Guardian
Mio, Michigan

Catherine Zimmerman
Trip Guardian
Royal Oak, Michigan

> "War is not a life; it is a situation, one which may neither be ignored nor accepted."
>
> – T.S. Eliot, Poet

Honor Flight 18 Saturday, October 18, 2008

More photos of this trip at www.honorflightmichigan.com

Eugene H. Arjeski
World War II Veteran
Grosse Pointe, Michigan

Paul T. Dost
World War II Veteran
Caro, Michigan

Edward Kochoian
World War II Veteran
Taylor, Michigan

Walter Napthen
World War II Veteran
Lake, Michigan

Herbert G. Smith
World War II Veteran
Warren, Michigan

Harrell L. Balch
World War II Veteran
Roseville, Michigan

Paul Festian
World War II Veteran
Caro, Michigan

William J. Kurth
World War II Veteran
Clinton Township, Michigan

Harry W. Patterson
World War II Veteran
Southgate, Michigan

George R. Stange
World War II Veteran
Southgate, Michigan

Gordon J. Bibby
World War II Veteran
Royal Oak, Michigan

Peter Ficorelli
World War II Veteran
Shelby Township, Michigan

John F. Laffey
World War II Veteran
Roseville, Michigan

Harold R. Quist
World War II Veteran
Livonia, Michigan

Jimmy Stefoff
World War II Veteran
Owosso, Michigan

Paul A. Buscemi
World War II Veteran
Clinton Township, Michigan

George H. Gerberding
World War II Veteran
Utica, Michigan

Joseph F. Marheineke
World War II Veteran
Clinton Township, Michigan

Ralph G. Quist
World War II Veteran
Southfield, Michigan

Justin Sutton
World War II Veteran
Hudson, Michigan

Robert W. Burk
World War II Veteran
Livonia, Michigan

Gerald A. Haeske
World War II Veteran
Saginaw, Michigan

John W. Megge
World War II Veteran
Fraser, Michigan

Edward A. Rabish
World War II Veteran
Pinconning, Michigan

John Vecchioni
World War II Veteran
Dearborn Heights, Michigan

Milton T. Charlebois
World War II Veteran
Harsens Island, Michigan

William A. Hannula
World War II Veteran
Southgate, Michigan

Elmer C. Meitzner
World War II Veteran
Utica, Michigan

Gordon J. Seedberg
World War II Veteran
Livonia, Michigan

Alfred C. Volante
World War II Veteran
Allen Park, Michigan

Arthur J. Ciechanowski
World War II Veteran
Roseville, Michigan

Sterling E. Hobson
World War II Veteran
Warren, Michigan

Paul C. Moellering
World War II Veteran
Plymouth, Michigan

Joseph P. Sheppard
World War II Veteran
Mt. Pleasant, Michigan

Karl H. Wagner
World War II Veteran
Manistee, Michigan

Arnold F. Dahlke
World War II Veteran
Roseville, Michigan

Harvey F. Holley
World War II Veteran
Allen Park, Michigan

Donald O. Morris
World War II Veteran
Fraser, Michigan

Edward S. Skiba
World War II Veteran
Roseville, Michigan

Edward T. Wlodarczyk
World War II Veteran
Roseville, Michigan

Ted Wross
World War II Veteran
Roseville, Michigan

Debra L. Keyes
Trip Guardian
Long Grove, Illinois

Carol A. Marcis
Trip Guardian
Taylor, Michigan

Ayleet "Bud" Wease
Trip Leader
Royal Oak, Michigan

Michael McCarthy
Trip Guardian
Southfield, Michigan

Chris Zimmel
Medical Personnel
Clawson, Michigan

Gary D. Megge
Trip Guardian
Warren, Michigan

Valerie A. Beckrow
Trip Guardian
Caro, Michigan

Don O. Morris
Trip Guardian
Kalamazoo, Michigan

Edward Burkhardt
Trip Guardian
Royal Oak, Michigan

David E. Napthen
Trip Guardian
Warren, Michigan

Cynthia Canty
Trip Guardian
Birmingham, Michigan

Pamela Robbins
Trip Guardian
Royal Oak, Michigan

Angela M. DeBrincat
Trip Guardian
Lake Orion, Michigan

Karl S. Wagner
Trip Guardian
Troy, Michigan

"Thanks again for all you are doing for us World War II veterans. Sometimes it seems like we are not only the "Greatest Generation" but also the "Forgotten Generation". Keep up the good work and express my thanks to all those who were our escorts."

– Proud World War II Veteran
Honor Flight Michigan Alumnus

Honor Flight 19 Saturday, November 1, 2008
More photos of this trip at www.honorflightmichigan.com

Harry T. Adams World War II Veteran Waterford, Michigan	**Eugene Dalbo** World War II Veteran Allen Park, Michigan	**John T. Kirchhoff** World War II Veteran Detroit, Michigan	**John P. Murphy** World War II Veteran Benton Harbor, Michigan	**Donald E. Ulbrich** World War II Veteran Detroit, Michigan
Francis Alexander World War II Veteran Port Huron, Michigan	**Arthur L. DeBres** World War II Veteran Allegan, Michigan	**Ernest H. Klimek** World War II Veteran Livonia, Michigan	**Murillo J. Murri** World War II Veteran St. Clair Shores, Michigan	
Roland G. Arndt World War II Veteran Farmington Hills, Michigan	**Frank Depolo** World War II Veteran Inkster, Michigan	**Thomas L. Kopke** World War II Veteran Dearborn, Michigan	**Mac N. Petteys** World War II Veteran Millington, Michigan	**Richard P. Sage** Trip Leader Royal Oak, Michigan
Milton L. Baker World War II Veteran Westland, Michigan	**John T. Eschels** World War II Veteran Birmingham, Michigan	**Fred Lax** World War II Veteran Ferndale, Michigan	**A.J. Pike** World War II Veteran Howell, Michigan	**Patrick G. Benson** Medical Personnel Imlay City, Michigan
Walter S. Bala World War II Veteran Southfield, Michigan	**Andrew F. Fritz** World War II Veteran St. Clair Shores, Michigan	**William J. McMillan** World War II Veteran Frankfort, Michigan	**Eugene V. Small** World War II Veteran Livonia, Michigan	**John E. Kirchhoff** Medical Personnel New Baltimore, Michigan
John B. Barr World War II Veteran Plymouth, Michigan	**Angelo Gatteri** World War II Veteran Westland, Michigan	**Lewis H. Mead** World War II Veteran Byron Center, Michigan	**Benedict J. Smith** World War II Veteran Birmingham, Michigan	**Carolyn M. Reidel** Medical Personnel Clinton Township, Michigan
Leonard Budzen World War II Veteran Highland, Michigan	**Nathaniel James** World War II Veteran Detroit, Michigan	**Christopher Melikan** World War II Veteran Melvindale, Michigan	**Alfred S. Szandzik** World War II Veteran St. Clair Shores, Michigan	**Brad P. Ziegler** Official Photographer West Bloomfield, Michigan
Kenneth W. Croner World War II Veteran Grand Blanc, Michigan	**Waine D. Kanack** World War II Veteran Farmington, Michigan	**Stanley E. Metiva** World War II Veteran Saginaw, Michigan	**Jack W. Taylor** World War II Veteran Alanson, Michigan	**Edward R. Alexander** Trip Guardian Port Huron, Michigan

Catherine M. Beaumont
Trip Guardian
Royal Oak, Michigan

Curran M. McCarthy
Trip Guardian
Royal Oak, Michigan

John W. Campbell
Trip Guardian
Byron Center, Michigan

Christine K. Oglesbee
Trip Guardian
Allegan, Michigan

Antoinette M. Frawley
Trip Guardian
Shelby Township, Michigan

Joseph E. Rosinski
Trip Guardian
Clarkston, Michigan

Margaret M. Gatteri
Trip Guardian
Westland, Michigan

Frank A. Ruzicka
Trip Guardian
Auburn Hills, Michigan

Debra J. Hollis
Trip Guardian
Royal Oak, Michigan

Maureen E. Sage
Trip Guardian
Royal Oak, Michigan

Carol Kavanaugh-Burgess
Trip Guardian
Warren, Michigan

Ardel M. Schmidt
Trip Guardian
Westland, Michigan

Gary L. Laniewicz
Trip Guardian
Prudenville, Michigan

Mark B. Stevens
Trip Guardian
Jackson, Michigan

Sandra L. Lupu
Trip Guardian
Eastpointe, Michigan

Matthew W. Yardley
Trip Guardian
Livonia, Michigan

" What we have done for ourselves alone dies with us; what we have done for others and the world remains and is immortal. "

– Albert Pike – American Poet – Confederate Soldier

Honor Flight 20

Saturday, November 15, 2008
More photos of this trip at www.honorflightmichigan.com

William H. Anderson
World War II Veteran
Royal Oak, Michigan

John J. Dennis
World War II Veteran
Brownstown, Michigan

John W. Kerastas
World War II Veteran
Farmington Hills, Michigan

John Malak
World War II Veteran
Shelby Township, Michigan

Johnnie Richmond
World War II Veteran
Dearborn, Michigan

Donald W. Aupperle
World War II Veteran
Fraser, Michigan

Donald L. Dipboye
World War II Veteran
Sterling Heights, Michigan

George H. Koehler
World War II Veteran
Inkster, Michigan

Frank Marschall
World War II Veteran
Southgate, Michigan

George R. Rossbach
World War II Veteran
Oxford, Michigan

Frank D. Barber
World War II Veteran
Farmington, Michigan

James T. Forbes
World War II Veteran
Farmington Hills, Michigan

Joseph H. Kohler
World War II Veteran
Sterling Heights, Michigan

Alfonzo O. Massey
World War II Veteran
Detroit, Michigan

Roy D. Schneider
World War II Veteran
Commerce Township, Michigan

Thomas M. Barrett
World War II Veteran
Madison Heights, Michigan

Charles W. Gall
World War II Veteran
Owosso, Michigan

Chester J. Kolo
World War II Veteran
Livonia, Michigan

Donald H. Metro
World War II Veteran
Berkley, Michigan

Edward A. Steiner
World War II Veteran
Taylor, Michigan

Richard L. Borges
World War II Veteran
Garden City, Michigan

Christine M. Gavrila
World War II Veteran
Bay City, Michigan

Andrew Kominsky
World War II Veteran
Shelby Township, Michigan

Wilbur J. Miller
World War II Veteran
Taylor, Michigan

Al Stone
World War II Veteran
Ann Arbor, Michigan

George C. Buckley
World War II Veteran
St. Clair Shores, Michigan

Myron Handelsman
World War II Veteran
West Bloomfield, Michigan

Leslie J. Lowe
World War II Veteran
Farmington Hills, Michigan

Peter P. Morici
World War II Veteran
Harper Woods, Michigan

Donald B. Trumble
World War II Veteran
Northville, Michigan

John B. Campbell
World War II Veteran
Royal Oak, Michigan

Ellis L. Hicks
World War II Veteran
Prudenville, Michigan

Dolores M. Maillette
World War II Veteran
Bay City, Michigan

Alan L. Reade
World War II Veteran
Bloomfield Hills, Michigan

Lorraine A. Waling
World War II Veteran
Livonia, Michigan

August F. Cipponeri
World War II Veteran
Clinton Township, Michigan

Adam J. Jadczak
World War II Veteran
Livonia, Michigan

Robert F. Maks
World War II Veteran
Sterling Heights, Michigan

Eugene Richardson
World War II Veteran
Howell, Michigan

Victor V. Waling
World War II Veteran
Livonia, Michigan

Richard P. Sage
Trip Leader
Royal Oak, Michigan

Rozanne L. Jacques
Medical Personnel
St.Clair Shores, Michigan

Nancy A. Malak
Medical Personnel
Rochester Hills, Michigan

Nate Strong
Official Photographer
Wixom, Michigan

Edward Burkhardt
Trip Guardian
Royal Oak, Michigan

Diane Gabil
Trip Guardian
Essexville, Michigan

Thomas N. Gall
Trip Guardian
Corunna, Michigan

Thomas E. Hoff
Trip Guardian
Royal Oak, Michigan

Joseph T. Kohler
Trip Guardian
Lake Orion, Michigan

Pauline A. Kulwicki
Trip Guardian
Clinton Township, Michigan

Michael J. Maillette
Trip Guardian
Bay City, Michigan

Joan M. Richardson
Trip Guardian
Howell, Michigan

Maureen E. Sage
Trip Guardian
Royal Oak, Michigan

Nancy Walters
Trip Guardian
Royal Oak, Michigan

Ronald R. Walters
Trip Guardian
Royal Oak, Michigan

" Thank you Dave Cameron and Honor Flight for never forgetting about us. Our trip was too wonderful to put into words with every detail attended to with military precision. Bless you all. "

– Proud World War II Veteran
Honor Flight Michigan Alumnus

Honor Flight 21 Saturday, April 11, 2009
More photos of this trip at www.honorflightmichigan.com

Edwin C. Barnhart	Donald D. Clark	Eugene C. Karbowski	Norbert Przybylski	James M. Staton
World War II Veteran	World War II Veteran	World War II Veteran	World War II Veteran	World War II Veteran
Romeo, Michigan	Deerfield, Michigan	Auburn, Michigan	Heiskell, Tennessee	Warren, Michigan
Alfredo R. Bicego	Alfred P. Debski	Howard L. Keefer	Richard A. Przybylski	Henry A. Szyndlar
World War II Veteran	World War II Veteran	World War II Veteran	World War II Veteran	World War II Veteran
Troy, Michigan	St. Clair Shores, Michigan	Three Oaks, Michigan	Allen Park, Michigan	Warren, Michigan
Kenneth M. Bittner	Earl N. Elliott	William W. Killebrew	Oscar D. Puryear	George Tirakian
World War II Veteran	World War II Veteran	World War II Veteran	World War II Veteran	World War II Veteran
Royal Oak, Michigan	Wingham, Ontario, Canada	Grosse Pointe Woods, Michigan	Frankenmuth, Michigan	Warren, Michigan
Leon Bleifeld	Joseph A. Golaszewski	Bernard S. Litt	William J. Schafer	Daniel J. Valko
World War II Veteran	World War II Veteran	World War II Veteran	World War II Veteran	World War II Veteran
Oak Park, Michigan	Warren, Michigan	West Bloomfield, Michigan	Beverly Hills, Michigan	Pontiac, Michigan
Lewis R. Bone	John A. Hastedt	Harold V. Miller	Lyle E. Schlappi	John R. Vallad
World War II Veteran	World War II Veteran	World War II Veteran	World War II Veteran	World War II Veteran
Flat Rock, Michigan	Grand Blanc, Michigan	Farmington Hills, Michigan	Ludington, Michigan	St. Clair Shores, Michigan
Robert R. Cave	Jackson L. Henderson	George K. Mugianis	Andrew A. Seleno	Omer J. Van Huylenbrouck
World War II Veteran	World War II Veteran	World War II Veteran	World War II Veteran	World War II Veteran
Warren, Michigan	Shelby Township, Michigan	Southfield, Michigan	Troy, Michigan	Royal Oak, Michigan
William F. Charles	Thomas N. Jacks	Robert P. Owen	Donald G. Skrzycki	George S. Veach
World War II Veteran	World War II Veteran	World War II Veteran	World War II Veteran	World War II Veteran
Flint, Michigan	Oak Park, Michigan	Livonia, Michigan	Taylor, Michigan	Wayne, Michigan
Paul Cicchini	John Kalfaian	Edmund Pluta	Robert B. Smith	Jack D. Virga
World War II Veteran	World War II Veteran	World War II Veteran	World War II Veteran	World War II Veteran
Bloomfield Hills, Michigan	Warren, Michigan	Flint, Michigan	Tucson, Arizonia	Clinton Township, Michigan

Cynthia A. Gumpert
Trip Guardian
Buchanan, Michigan

Richard P. Sage
Trip Leader
Royal Oak, Michigan

David C. Jencks
Trip Guardian
Pleasant Ridge, Michigan

Connie M. MacDowell
Medical Personnel
Waterford, Michigan

Virginia S. Neal
Trip Guardian
Mason, Ohio

Christine Zimmel
Medical Personnel
Clawson, Michigan

Paul E. Skrzycki
Trip Guardian
Belleville, Michigan

Brad P. Ziegler
Official Photographer
West Bloomfield, Michigan

George L. Tirakian
Trip Guardian
Madison Heights, Michigan

Dale J. Bone
Trip Guardian
Flat Rock, Michigan

Janice L. Yannello
Trip Guardian
Clarkston, Michigan

Michael R. Cave
Trip Guardian
Bloomfield Hills, Michigan

Marie Zalucki
Trip Guardian
Sterling Heights, Michigan

Debra S. Drummond
Trip Guardian
Livonia, Michigan

Catherine L. Zimmerman
Trip Guardian
Royal Oak, Michigan

“ I hate war as only a soldier who has lived it can, only as one who has seen its brutality, its stupidity. ”

– General Dwight D. Eisenhower

Honor Flight 22 Saturday, April 25, 2009
More photos of this trip at www.honorflightmichigan.com

Vernon E. Bublitz	Francis P. Farney	Leonard G. Hendricks	Francis M. Robison	Thomas J. Zachary
World War II Veteran	World War II Veteran	World War II Veteran	World War II Veteran	World War II Veteran
Bad Axe, Michigan	Mt. Morris, Michigan	Auburn Hills, Michigan	Northville, Michigan	Royal Oak, Michigan
Alvin E. Buss	Thomas J. Farney	Gordon A. Howcroft	Richard R. Rogers	
World War II Veteran	World War II Veteran	World War II Veteran	World War II Veteran	
Prudenville, Michigan	Flushing, Michigan	New Baltimore, Michigan	Bellaire, Michigan	
Roger J. Buysse	Harvey S. Fournier	Charles L. James	Leon C. Steenbergh	Pamela Robbins
World War II Veteran	World War II Veteran	World War II Veteran	World War II Veteran	Trip Leader
St. Clair Shores, Michigan	Escanaba, Michigan	Clarkston, Michigan	East Jordan, Michigan	Royal Oak, Michigan

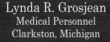

Lynda R. Grosjean
Medical Personnel
Clarkston, Michigan

David Phillips
Trip Guardian
Clarkston, Michigan

Nate Strong
Official Photographer
Wixom, Michigan

Suzanne J. Robison
Trip Guardian
Novi, Michigan

Carolyn R. Bloom
Trip Guardian
West Bloomfield, Michigan

Penny Rogers
Trip Guardian
Bellaire, Michigan

Norman J. Cormier
Trip Guardian
Dearborn Heights, Michigan

Robert P. Stonik
Trip Guardian
Brighton, Michigan

Linda M. Corriveau
Trip Guardian
Leonard, Michigan

Ayleet "Bud" Wease
Trip Guardian
Royal Oak, Michigan

Kathleen A. Evers
Trip Guardian
South Lyon, Michigan

Calvin W. Wilkinson
Trip Guardian
Royal Oak, Michigan

Eric E. Hakel
Trip Guardian
Otisville, Michigan

Carol J. Zirotte
Trip Guardian
Oak Park, Michigan

David M. Howcroft
Trip Guardian
Armada, Michigan

> "Without Honor Flight Michigan, I along with so many other veterans of WWII would never have had the opportunity to see our memorial. The entire day was just more than I could comprehend. I truly feel honored but mostly grateful."
>
> – Proud World War II Veteran
> Honor Flight Michigan Alumnus

Honor Flight 23 Saturday, May 9, 2009

More photos of this trip at www.honorflightmichigan.com

Anthony E. Badaglialacqua
World War II Veteran
Shelby Township, Michigan

Richard T. Boris
World War II Veteran
Madison Heights, Michigan

Charles L. Holden
World War II Veteran
Stevensville, Michigan

Dwight S. Lewis
World War II Veteran
Green Oak Township, Michigan

Cleo F. Prescott
World War II Veteran
Vermontville, Michigan

Robert R. Ballard
World War II Veteran
Waterford, Michigan

Robert R. Dedrich
World War II Veteran
Warren, Michigan

Joseph A. Hulway
World War II Veteran
Clinton Township, Michigan

Martin T. McKee
World War II Veteran
Grosse Pointe Woods, Michigan

Raymond L. Redmond
World War II Veteran
Clinton Township, Michigan

Milton Barach
World War II Veteran
Roseville, Michigan

George R. Dodson
World War II Veteran
Plymouth, Michigan

George F. Kalamas
World War II Veteran
Southgate, Michigan

James J. Mulligan
World War II Veteran
Rochester, Michigan

Roy K. Scites
World War II Veteran
Warren, Michigan

Steve E. Baynai
World War II Veteran
Riverview, Michigan

Carl W. Eich
World War II Veteran
Saginaw, Michigan

Robert E. Kegler
World War II Veteran
Northville, Michigan

John F. Nerowski
World War II Veteran
Wyandotte, Michigan

Jerome J. Sharafinski
World War II Veteran
Clinton Township, Michigan

Joseph J. Bednarczyk
World War II Veteran
Lexington, Michigan

Raymond L. Evans
World War II Veteran
Grosse Pointe Farms, Michigan

Imojean Ketter
World War II Veteran
Waterford, Michigan

George Ouvry
World War II Veteran
Mancelona, Michigan

Thomas Solomon
World War II Veteran
Grosse Pointe Woods, Michigan

Roman Belobradich
World War II Veteran
Farmington, Michigan

Kenneth French
World War II Veteran
Clarkston, Michigan

Harold R. Knoll
World War II Veteran
St.Clair Shores, Michigan

Albert T. Paglia
World War II Veteran
Grosse Pointe, Michigan

Theodore M. Waligora
World War II Veteran
Sterling Heights, Michigan

John Bernard
World War II Veteran
Riverview, Michigan

Joseph G. Gagnon
World War II Veteran
Chesterfield, Michigan

James M. Kolka
World War II Veteran
Grayling, Michigan

Gus F. Pappas
World War II Veteran
Walled Lake, Michigan

John L. Warr
World War II Veteran
Detroit, Michigan

Joseph F. Boris
World War II Veteran
Stanwood, Michigan

Alexander G. Gulis
World War II Veteran
Bloomfield Hills, Michigan

Norbert F. Leszczynski
World War II Veteran
West Bloomfield, Michigan

Peter J. Pappas
World War II Veteran
Riverview, Michigan

Ralph White
World War II Veteran
Marysville, Michigan

Edmond R. Carleton
Trip Guardian
Lexington, Michigan

Richard P. Sage
Trip Leader
Royal Oak, Michigan

Lori A. Drumm
Trip Guardian
Brownstown, Michigan

Theresa A. Badaglialacqua
Medical Personnel
Birmingham, Michigan

Debra J. Hollis
Trip Guardian
Royal Oak, Michigan

Susan M. Jones
Medical Personnel
Greenwood Township, Michigan

Mari A. Martin
Trip Guardian
Charlotte, Michigan

Brad P. Ziegler
Official Photographer
West Bloomfield, Michigan

Jan K. McCann
Trip Guardian
West Bloomfield, Michigan

Susan E. Adent
Trip Guardian
Baroda, Michigan

Michael McCarthy
Trip Guardian
Southfield, Michigan

Michael D. Burton
Trip Guardian
Grand Rapids, Michigan

Gary C. Ouvry
Trip Guardian
Mt. Pleasant, Michigan

Michael Cameron
Trip Guardian
Farmington Hills, Michigan

Dustin C. Rice
Trip Guardian
East Lansing, Michigan

" There's no honorable way to kill, no gentle way to destroy. There is nothing good in war except its ending. "

– President Abraham Lincoln

Honor Flight 24 Saturday, August 22, 2009
More photos of this trip at www.honorflightmichigan.com

25

Ernest G. Aruffo
World War II Veteran
Novi, Michigan

Walter Drenth
World War II Veteran
Grand Rapids, Michigan

Bennie Krupa
World War II Veteran
Bay City, Michigan

James S. Roye
World War II Veteran
Livonia, Michigan

Stuart P. Weckerly
World War II Veteran
Dearborn, Michigan

Peter Bilovus
World War II Veteran
Troy, Michigan

David W. Edwards
World War II Veteran
Waterford, Michigan

John C. Malejan
World War II Veteran
Hartland, Michigan

Joseph E. Salva
World War II Veteran
Lapeer, Michigan

Peter White
World War II Veteran
Novi, Michigan

George Binson
World War II Veteran
Madison Heights, Michigan

Raymond W. Fleisher
World War II Veteran
West Bloomfield, Michigan

William W. McKettrick
World War II Veteran
West Bloomfield, Michigan

John F. Sojka
World War II Veteran
Grayling, Michigan

Robert L. Willard
World War II Veteran
Buchanan, Michigan

Ernest L. Bockstanz
World War II Veteran
Kalamazoo, Michigan

Eugene S. Hoiby
World War II Veteran
Livonia, Michigan

Robert F. Morris
World War II Veteran
Waterford, Michigan

Frederick Steerzer
World War II Veteran
Chesterfield Township, Michigan

James M. Wilson
World War II Veteran
Harper Woods, Michigan

Maxwell W. Brown
World War II Veteran
Bay City, Michigan

Gordon F. Hubbert
World War II Veteran
Charlotte, Michigan

Charles T. Myer
World War II Veteran
Trenton, Michigan

William J. Steerzer
World War II Veteran
Riley, Michigan

Gerald G. Ziel
World War II Veteran
Flint, Michigan

Roy Bultman
World War II Veteran
Grand Rapids, Michigan

Dellis W. Hudson
World War II Veteran
Port Huron, Michigan

William T. Patton
World War II Veteran
Temperance, Michigan

Louis F. Truna
World War II Veteran
Erie, Michigan

Lawrence A. Zipp
World War II Veteran
Charlevoix, Michigan

Robert J. Butler
World War II Veteran
Lake Orion, Michigan

Elton O. Jobse
World War II Veteran
Macomb, Michigan

Norma G. Rambow
World War II Veteran
Battle Creek, Michigan

Dirk B. Waltz
World War II Veteran
Midland, Michigan

_____

Bruce A. Caswell
World War II Veteran
Holly, Michigan

Frank L. Kidder
World War II Veteran
Oxford, Michigan

Edward F. Rettig
World War II Veteran
Clarkston, Michigan

Robert L. Wayland
World War II Veteran
Grosse Pointe Woods, Michigan

Charles J. Peltier
Trip Leader
South Lyon, Michigan

Vallie G. McColley
Medical Personnel
Midland, Michigan

Chris Zimmel
Medical Personnel
Clawson, Michigan

Nate Strong
Official Photorapher
Wixom, Michigan

James W. Copping
Trip Guardian
Port Huron, Michigan

George A. Daves
Trip Guardian
Plymouth, Michigan

Melissa Downey
Trip Guardian
Huntington Woods, Michigan

Timothy Downey
Trip Guardian
Huntington Woods, Michigan

Ronald J. Hefner
Trip Guardian
Plattsmouth, Nebraska

Alan J. Muskovitz
Trip Guardian
West Bloomfield, Michigan

Daniel J. Muskovitz
Trip Guardian
West Bloomfield, Michigan

Janice M. Posadny
Trip Guardian
Temperance, Michigan

Jeffrey M. Rust
Trip Guardian
China Township, Michigan

Larry A. Strong
Trip Guardian
Evart, Michigan

"Providing this memorable gift to all World War II veterans, now in their 80's, some very fragile, is most generous and compassionate. It is with sincere thanks for my trip that I enclose this check so that another World War II veteran can get a chance to go before it is too late."

– Proud World War II Veteran
Honor Flight Michigan Alumnus

Honor Flight 25 Saturday, October 10, 2009
More photos of this trip at www.honorflightmichigan.com

Ernest Bastianelli	Alfred Elders	Matthew B. Hrabosky	Raymond F. McPartlin	Arthur J. Snook
World War II Veteran	World War II Veteran	World War II Veteran	World War II Veteran	World War II Veteran
Warren, Michigan	Grandville, Michigan	Belleville, Michigan	Bloomfield Hills, Michigan	Warren, Michigan
Joseph A. Bommarito	Lewis Elders	John J. Keenan	Donald R. Perkins	Donald N. Stevenson
World War II Veteran	World War II Veteran	World War II Veteran	World War II Veteran	World War II Veteran
Clinton Township, Michigan	Grandville, Michigan	Bloomfield Hills, Michigan	Allegan, Michigan	Plymouth, Michigan
William C. Brown	James M. Ferguson	Malcolm Keteian	Theodore J. Potok	Jerome J. Wilkins
World War II Veteran	World War II Veteran	World War II Veteran	World War II Veteran	World War II Veteran
Northville, Michigan	Rochester Hills, Michigan	Sterling Heights, Michigan	Livonia, Michigan	Roseville, Michigan
Harold B. Casey	Henry B. Goodwin	Vayden King	Edward J. Prchlik	Stanley P. Wilkins
World War II Veteran	World War II Veteran	World War II Veteran	World War II Veteran	World War II Veteran
Swartz Creek, Michigan	Lathrup Village, Michigan	Warren, Michigan	Swartz Creek, Michigan	Farmington, Michigan
John M. Cirelle	Donald C. Gorman	John Kissel	Joseph S. Rusin	Cecil F. Willingham
World War II Veteran	World War II Veteran	World War II Veteran	World War II Veteran	World War II Veteran
St. Clair Shores, Michigan	Novi, Michigan	Dearborn, Michigan	Sterling Heights, Michigan	South Lyon, Michigan
Charles T. Cooke	Douglas J. Harvey	Elmer Lundeen	William L. Schlaud	Fred J. Wolff
World War II Veteran	World War II Veteran	World War II Veteran	World War II Veteran	World War II Veteran
Jackson, Michigan	Sterling Heights, Michigan	Detroit, Michigan	North Branch, Michigan	Redford, Michigan

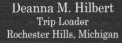

26

Karla S. Halvangis
Trip Guardian
Novi, Michigan

Deanna M. Hilbert
Trip Loader
Rochester Hills, Michigan

Kip E. Hilbert
Trip Guardian
Rochester Hills, Michigan

Walter Groesbeck
Medical Personnel
Oxford, Michigan

Carol Kavanaugh-Burgess
Trip Guardian
Warren, Michigan

Lori E. Lockwood
Medical Personnel
Waterford, Michigan

Thomas A. King
Trip Guardian
Washington Township, Michigan

Michael J. Remley
Medical Personnel
Clarkston, Michigan

Virginia E. Moore
Trip Guardian
Mt. Clemens, Michigan

Brad P. Ziegler
Official Photographer
West Bloomfield, Michigan

Steven C. Stanford
Trip Guardian
Howell, Michigan

Catherine A. Kavanaugh
Press - Media
Dearborn, Michigan

Marlene S. Violassi
Trip Guardian
Bloomfield Hills, Michigan

James L. Ferguson
Trip Guardian
Waterford, Michigan

Jan L. Williams
Trip Guardian
Royal Oak, Michigan

> "Never in the field of human conflict was so much owed by so many to so few."
>
> – Sir Winston Churchill

Honor Flight 26 Saturday, October 24, 2009

More photos of this trip at www.honorflightmichigan.com

Stanley H. Berlin	Robert W. Dolmage	Thomas W. Millard	Oliver Schroeder	
World War II Veteran	World War II Veteran	World War II Veteran	World War II Veteran	_____
West Bloomfield, Michigan	Rochester Hills, Michigan	Hillman, Michigan	Bloomfield Hills, Michigan	
Dante H. Bessolo	Lyle R. Guenther	Robert J. Muir	Stanley D. Sczechowski	Debra J. Hollis
World War II Veteran	World War II Veteran	World War II Veteran	World War II Veteran	Trip Leader
Byron, Michigan	Caro, Michigan	Farmington Hills, Michigan	Troy, Michigan	Royal Oak, Michigan
Robert H. Bronsted	Paul F. Henning	Leonard F. Nancarrow	Raymond Shafer	Julie A. Thams
World War II Veteran	World War II Veteran	World War II Veteran	World War II Veteran	Medical Personnel
Rochester Hills, Michigan	Lansing, Michigan	Rochester Hills, Michigan	Lincoln Park, Michigan	Clarkston, Michigan
Andrew Coubrough	William J. Jenner	Harry Repoz	Russell R. Shields	Nate Strong
World War II Veteran	World War II Veteran	World War II Veteran	World War II Veteran	Official Photographer
Troy, Michigan	Wyandotte, Michigan	Royal Oak, Michigan	St. Clair Shores, Michigan	Wixom, Michigan

27

Dale L. Bargeron
Trip Guardian
Clarkston, Michigan

June E. Nagle
Trip Guardian
Waterford, Michigan

Joann F. Brown
Trip Guardian
Farmington Hills, Michigan

Kathleen M. Olson
Trip Guardian
Kentwood, Michigan

Edmond Burkhardt
Trip Guardian
Royal Oak, Michigan

Thomas M. Piasta
Trip Guardian
Canton, Michigan

Joellen Burton
Trip Guardian
Rochester Hills, Michigan

Tom R. Ramsey
Trip Guardian
Rochester Hills, Michigan

Kathy Dorsey
Trip Guardian
Ann Arbor, Michigan

Larry J. Repoz
Trip Guardian
Livonia, Michigan

John W. Glace
Trip Guardian
Ferndale, Michigan

Barbara J. Toman
Trip Guardian
Lansing, Michigan

Harry L. Kettler
Trip Guardian
Chesterfield, Michigan

James B. Winter
Trip Guardian
Clarkston, Michigan

Wendy H. Kibat
Trip Guardian
Troy, Michigan

Scott M. Yost
Trip Guardian
Kalkaska, Michigan

"Above all, we must realize that no arsenal, or no weapon in the arsenals of the world, is so formidable as the will and moral courage of free men and women. It is a weapon our adversaries in today's world do not have."

– President Ronald Reagan

Honor Flight 27 Saturday, November 7, 2009
More photos of this trip at www.honorflightmichigan.com

Eldon K. Andrews
World War II Veteran
Novi, Michigan

William H. Fritts
World War II Veteran
Macomb Township, Michigan

Robert R. Jurn
World War II Veteran
Imlay City, Michigan

Stuart L. Pagel
World War II Veteran
Northville, Michigan

Robert J. Siedlik
World War II Veteran
Livonia, Michigan

Edmund A. Aubrey
World War II Veteran
St. Clair Shores, Michigan

Augustus G. Ganakas
World War II Veteran
East Lansing, Michigan

Francis E. Keenan
World War II Veteran
Westland, Michigan

Bernard A. Picotte
World War II Veteran
Novi, Michigan

Douglas D. Steiger
World War II Veteran
Rochester Hills, Michigan

Lynn H. Barber
World War II Veteran
Novi, Michigan

Charles H. Goebel
World War II Veteran
Novi, Michigan

Rudolph R. Kuzma
World War II Veteran
Dearborn Heights, Michigan

Robert E. Pierce
World War II Veteran
Oxford, Michigan

Donald R. Switzer
World War II Veteran
Osseo, Michigan

Lewis G. Bartlett
World War II Veteran
Novi, Michigan

Frank J. Gorniak
World War II Veteran
Novi, Michigan

Robert E. McAvoy
World War II Veteran
Owosso, Michigan

Erwin V. Porath
World War II Veteran
Sterling, Michigan

Ray B. Van Voorthuysen
World War II Veteran
Muskegon, Michigan

Eugene N. Buel
World War II Veteran
Marine City, Michigan

Earl F. Hagstrom
World War II Veteran
Burton, Michigan

James A. McFalda
World War II Veteran
Presque Isle, Michigan

Edward J. Pritchard
World War II Veteran
Novi, Michigan

Edward J. Williams
World War II Veteran
Ann Arbor, Michigan

Joseph A. Dutts
World War II Veteran
St. Clair Shores, Michigan

Stanley T. Hirozawa
World War II Veteran
Novi, Michigan

Gabriel Michel
World War II Veteran
Sterling Heights, Michigan

Burton J. Schimpke
World War II Veteran
Novi, Michigan

Floyd E. Wiseley
World War II Veteran
Marine City, Michigan

William F. Emrick
World War II Veteran
Novi, Michigan

Sylvester J. Jaye
World War II Veteran
Novi, Michigan

Richard S. Miles
World War II Veteran
Novi, Michigan

Charles R. Shafer
World War II Veteran
Novi, Michigan

Alfred Witt
World War II Veteran
Rochester Hills, Michigan

Robert A. Finn
World War II Veteran
Northville, Michigan

Joseph B. Jefferies
World War II Veteran
Redford, Michigan

Walter W. Moore
World War II Veteran
Canton, Michigan

Nellie P. Shafer
World War II Veteran
Novi, Michigan

James M. Wolfe
World War II Veteran
Harrison Township, Michigan

Richard P. Sage
Trip Leader
Royal Oak, Michigan

Rebecca M. Navarrette
Medical Personnel
St. Clair Shores, Michigan

William A. Schimpke
Medical Personnel
Lake Angelus, Michigan

Dennis J. Martineau
Official Photographer
Canton, Michigan

Jeremy J. Allnut
Trip Guardian
Bowling Green, Ohio

Carole Cameron
Trip Guardian
West Bloomfield, Michigan

Michael Cameron
Trip Guardian
Farmington Hills, Michigan

Joyce J. Fulgenzi
Trip Guardian
Lapeer, Michigan

James S. Guc
Trip Guardian
Cass City, Michigan

Christopher J. Hass
Trip Guardian
Rochester Hills, Michigan

Joseph M. Hass
Trip Guardian
Rochester Hills, Michigan

Patrick A. McFalda
Trip Guardian
Clarkston, Michigan

Dennis D. Schultz
Trip Guardian
Royal Oak, Michigan

Ayleet "Bud" Wease
Trip Guardian
Royal Oak, Michigan

Deborah Wease
Trip Guardian
Royal Oak, Michigan

"We were accompanied by 12 Guardian volunteers who took care of 8 wheelchair-bound veterans and guided us through the logistics of the all-day tour. They paid their own way for the opportunity to serve us. They are heroes as well."

– Proud World War II Veteran
Honor Flight Michigan Alumnus

Honor Flight 28 Saturday, November 14, 2009

More photos of this trip at www.honorflightmichigan.com

Bernard G. Bovee World War II Veteran Cadillac, Michigan	**James A. Gallagher** World War II Veteran Lansing, Michigan	**Michael J. Keegan** World War II Veteran Grosse Pointe Woods, Michigan	**Robert L. Pulsifer** World War II Veteran Muskegon, Michigan	**Raymond A. Walter** World War II Veteran Newaygo, Michigan
Fred Brauning World War II Veteran St. Clair Shores, Michigan	**Zigmund R. Gron** World War II Veteran Macomb, Michigan	**Henry O. Krans** World War II Veteran Iron River, Michigan	**Emil L. Salay** World War II Veteran Burton, Michigan	**Herbert E. Way** World War II Veteran Grand Rapids, Michigan
Robert L. Bush World War II Veteran Flint, Michigan	**Charles A. Harman** World War II Veteran Davison, Michigan	**Roger L. Kyle** World War II Veteran Northville, Michigan	**Teddy J. Schmidt** World War II Veteran Unionville, Michigan	**Thomas J. Young** World War II Veteran Brighton, Michigan
Walter F. Camp World War II Veteran Muskegon, Michigan	**Casper E. Hatmaker** World War II Veteran Gregory, Michigan	**Leo W. LeTourneau** World War II Veteran Bay City, Michigan	**Richard J. Schneider** World War II Veteran Northville, Michigan	**Edward L. Yuhas** World War II Veteran Clawson, Michigan
Earle A. Chorbagian World War II Veteran Canton, Michigan	**Daniel Hoffer** World War II Veteran West Bloomfield, Michigan	**Edward R. Matlock** World War II Veteran St. Clair Shores, Michigan	**Robert E. Schwartz** World War II Veteran West Bloomfield, Michigan	————
Leonard J. Cieslak World War II Veteran Gregory, Michigan	**Leo Hollander** World War II Veteran Farmington Hills, Michigan	**Steven H. Meyers** World War II Veteran Farmington Hills, Michigan	**Philip Toia** World War II Veteran Warren, Michigan	**Richard P. Sage** Trip Leader Royal Oak, Michigan
August C. Dorando World War II Veteran Farmington Hills, Michigan	**Norbert J. Kaminski** World War II Veteran Detroit, Michigan	**Edward T. Morrisette** World War II Veteran Mt. Clemens, Michigan	**Frank Train** World War II Veteran Temperance, Michigan	**Kenneth L. Bergsman** Medical Personnel Birmingham, Michigan
Donald J. Frisch World War II Veteran Oxford, Michigan	**Don R. Kebler** World War II Veteran Caro, Michigan	**Louis E. Piland** World War II Veteran Holt, Michigan	**Thomas N. Van Eyck** World War II Veteran Holland, Michigan	**Nate Strong** Official Photographer Wixom, Michigan

Linda C. Broling
Trip Guardian
Wanatah, Michigan

Gail C. Larke
Trip Guardian
Davison, Michigan

Edward Burkhardt
Trip Guardian
Royal Oak, Michigan

Michael E. LeTourneau
Trip Guardian
Indianapolis, Indiana

Cynthia Canty
Trip Guardian
Birmingham, Michigan

Alfred W. McLean
Trip Guardian
Roseville, Michigan

Bruce R. Findlay
Trip Guardian
Caro, Michigan

Sean J. O'Berski
Trip Guardian
Detroit, Michigan

Lana P. Gallagher
Trip Guardian
Lansing, Michigan

Amy S. Smith
Trip Guardian
Pinckney, Michigan

Barbara C. Hunter
Trip Guardian
Highland, Michigan

Sally L. Stevens
Trip Guardian
Flint, Michigan

Donald G. Hunter
Trip Guardian
Highland, Michigan

Rebecca L. VonMaluski
Trip Guardian
Lambertville, Michigan

Edward S. Krupinski
Trip Guardian
Warren, Michigan

Catherine L. Zimmerman
Trip Guardian
Royal Oak, Michigan

> "A hero is someone who understands the responsibility that comes with his freedom."
>
> – Bob Dylan, Singer-Songwriter

Honor Flight 29 Saturday, April 17, 2010

More photos of this trip at www.honorflightmichigan.com

Walter Berg World War II Veteran Rochester Hills, Michigan	**Chester Czubko** World War II Veteran Jackson, Michigan	**Edward W. Johnson** World War II Veteran Greenville, Michigan	**Clarence A. Rottmann** World War II Veteran Warren, Michigan	**Stanislaus Wojcik** World War II Veteran Chesterfield, Michigan
Heinze H. Blome World War II Veteran Farmington Hills, Michigan	**Garold W. Dean** World War II Veteran Gobles, Michigan	**Mae E. Johnson** World War II Veteran Greenville, Michigan	**Donald E. Ryerson** World War II Veteran Byron Center, Michigan	**Steven Ziemeck** World War II Veteran Paw Paw, Michigan
Edwin B. Bozian World War II Veteran West Bloomfield, Michigan	**Theodore E. Dice** World War II Veteran Milford, Michigan	**Donnie C. Kirk** World War II Veteran Jackson, Michigan	**Donald P. Saxon** World War II Veteran Rochester Hills, Michigan	————
Waldon C. Brand World War II Veteran Alden, Michigan	**August J. Edema** World War II Veteran Byron Center, Michigan	**Robert R. Kreger** World War II Veteran Jackson, Michigan	**Otto B. Scherf** World War II Veteran Dearborn, Michigan	**Deanna M. Hilbert** Trip Leader Rochester Hills, Michigan
John E. Case World War II Veteran Petoskey, Michigan	**Walter A. Fazer** World War II Veteran Powers, Michigan	**Bernard L. Krogel** World War II Veteran South Haven, Michigan	**Fred F. Schmitt** World War II Veteran Plymouth, Michigan	**Karen L. Wenzel** Medical Personnel Clarkston, Michigan
Francis E. Crawford World War II Veteran Oakland, Michigan	**Jack Fink** World War II Veteran Royal Oak, Michigan	**Kenneth F. Martin** World War II Veteran Roseville, Michigan	**William H. Schonberger** World War II Veteran Sterling Heights, Michigan	**Nate Strong** Official Photogrpaher Wixom, Michigan
John C. Crawford World War II Veteran Birmingham, Michigan	**Leo Golin** World War II Veteran Troy, Michigan	**Roy G. Poineau** World War II Veteran Saginaw, Michigan	**Harold F. Stevens** World War II Veteran Livonia, Michigan	**Edward Burkhardt** Trip Guardian Royal Oak, Michigan

30

Chester Czubko
Trip Guardian
Grass Lake, Michigan

Mary Beth Mayler
Trip Guardian
Dearborn, Michigan

Charles A. Zelinski
Trip Guardian
Clawson, Michigan

Bridget Demick
Trip Guardian
Washington, Michigan

Ronald Price
Trip Guardian
Orchard Lake, Michigan

David Dice
Trip Guardian
Bowling Green, Ohio

Kevin S. Rossiter
Trip Guardian
Royal Oak, Michigan

Maryann Golin
Trip Guardian
Troy, Michigan

Shirley A. Rottmann
Trip Guardian
Sterling Heights, Michigan

Dennis Hartman
Trip Guardian
Williston, Ohio

Timothy L. Tank
Trip Guardian
Graytown, Ohio

Katherine Hilbert
Trip Guardian
Rochester Hills, Michigan

Robert E. Teschendorf
Trip Guardian
Macomb, Michigan

Kip Hilbert
Trip Guardian
Rochester Hills, Michigan

Regina Ure
Trip Guardian
Troy, Michigan

John R. Kreger
Trip Guardian
Horton, Michigan

Norman Vansparrentak
Trip Guardian
Sterling Heights, Michigan

"The cost of freedom is always high, but Americans have always paid it. And one path we shall never choose, and that is the path of surrender, or submission."

– President John F. Kennedy

Honor Flight 30 Saturday, April 24, 2010
More photos of this trip at www.honorflightmichigan.com

Ralph S. Bennett
World War II Veteran
Highland, Michigan

Leonard D. Feerick
World War II Veteran
Sparta, Michigan

Gerard C. Lacey
World War II Veteran
Fenton, Michigan

Emil A. Przedwojewski
World War II Veteran
Ray, Michigan

Donald B. Vavra
World War II Veteran
Glen Arbor, Michigan

Thomas M. Breen
World War II Veteran
Shelby Township, Michigan

Joe F. Foos
World War II Veteran
Linden, Michigan

John E. Lammert
World War II Veteran
South Haven, Michigan

Bruno Przytakoski
World War II Veteran
Clawson, Michigan

Viva F. Williams
World War II Veteran
Marshall, Michigan

James Buchman
World War II Veteran
Harrison Township, Michigan

Cecil D. Gilbert
World War II Veteran
Shelby Township, Michigan

Richard W. Manos
World War II Veteran
Warren, Michigan

Herman R. Rindhage
World War II Veteran
Saginaw, Michigan

Harold J. Windorfer
World War II Veteran
Macomb, Michigan

Joseph G. Ceresia
World War II Veteran
Linden, Michigan

Arthur W. Gill
World War II Veteran
Stockbridge, Michigan

Irving Mendelson
World War II Veteran
West Bloomfield, Michigan

Arthur H. Rockensuess
World War II Veteran
St. Clair Shores, Michigan

————

Philip D'Agostino
World War II Veteran
Grosse Pointe Woods, Michigan

Cyril J. Glowinski
World War II Veteran
East Tawas City, Michigan

Irvin J. Moore
World War II Veteran
Ferndale, Michigan

Donald J. Schaffer
World War II Veteran
Flushing, Michigan

Debi Hollis
Trip Leader
Royal Oak, Michigan

Clarence H. Delor
World War II Veteran
Harper Woods, Michigan

Richard W. Kay
World War II Veteran
Grosse Pointe, Michigan

Edward Morren
World War II Veteran
Jenison, Michigan

Richard E. Schaft
World War II Veteran
Lapeer, Michigan

Lewis H. Rosenbaum
Medical Personnel
West Bloomfield, Michigan

Clarence A. Ennis
World War II Veteran
Brownstown, Michigan

Wilfred A. Kenward
World War II Veteran
Clinton Township, Michigan

Henri R. Nussbaum
World War II Veteran
Sterling Heights, Michigan

Wendell H. Semelroth
World War II Veteran
Troy, Michigan

Brad P. Ziegler
Official Photographer
West Bloomfield, Michigan

Frank Erdodi
World War II Veteran
Warren, Michigan

Robert K. Krotzer
World War II Veteran
Sterling Heights, Michigan

Joseph Placido
World War II Veteran
Southfield, Michigan

Ralph Vander Heide
World War II Veteran
Wyoming, Michigan

Jason Bennett
Trip Guardian
White Lake, Michigan

31

Michael Cameron
Trip Guardian
Farmington Hills, Michigan

Frederick E. Hollis
Trip Guardian
Bloomfield Hills, Michigan

Janet M. Elliott
Trip Guardian
Shelby Township, Michigan

Sally A. Jamison
Trip Guardian
Swartz Creek, Michigan

Suzanne C. Fleming
Trip Guardian
Naperville, Illinois

Barbara J. Lewinski
Trip Guardian
Marquette, Michigan

David J. Glowinski
Trip Guardian
Mikado, Michigan

Marc J. Mendelson
Trip Guardian
West Bloomfield, Michigan

Stephen G. Gordon
Trip Guardian
Royal Oak, Michigan

Daryl A. Miller
Trip Guardian
Fenton, Michigan

Andrea M. Harper
Trip Guardian
West Bloomfield, Michigan

Jack E. Morren
Trip Guardian
Caledonia, Michigan

Linda A. Helmick
Trip Guardian
South Lyon, Michigan

Heidi M. Smith
Trip Guardian
Canton, Michigan

Donna R. Hollis
Trip Guardian
Farmington, Michigan

Craig A. Strauss
Trip Guardian
Brownstown, Michigan

> "Women who stepped up were measured as citizens of the nation, not as women...This was a people's war, and everyone was in it."
>
> – Colonel Oveta Culp Hobby

Honor Flight 31
Saturday, May 1, 2010
More photos of this trip at www.honorflightmichigan.com

Stephen Bosanoz World War II Veteran Troy, Michigan	**Florian J. Gossler** World War II Veteran Decatur, Michigan	**John E. Lohrstorfer** World War II Veteran Battle Creek, Michigan	**Joseph M. Pletz** World War II Veteran Warren, Michigan	**Kenneth R. Van Nocker** World War II Veteran Okemos, Michigan
Donald J. Burzynski World War II Veteran Sterling Heights, Michigan	**Robert K. Gray** World War II Veteran Kalamazoo, Michigan	**Gordon Marshall** World War II Veteran Novi, Michigan	**Samuel N. Ray** World War II Veteran Novi, Michigan	**Antonio Vultaggio** World War II Veteran Warren, Michigan
Joseph J. Burzynski World War II Veteran Caseville, Michigan	**Richard W. Gregory** World War II Veteran Hamtramck, Michigan	**George B. Massora** World War II Veteran Decatur, Michigan	**Lowell W. Rutherford** World War II Veteran Battle Creek, Michigan	**James D. Walder** World War II Veteran Warren, Michigan
Gaspare C. Busuito World War II Veteran Shelby Township, Michigan	**Wayne K. Hellenga** World War II Veteran Decatur, Michigan	**Bruno G. Morelli** World War II Veteran Novi, Michigan	**James F. Schmitt** World War II Veteran Novi, Michigan	**Matthew J. Zipple** World War II Veteran Dearborn, Michigan
Arthur Carr World War II Veteran Washington, Michigan	**John A. Horne** World War II Veteran Novi, Michigan	**Alger J. Nielsen** World War II Veteran Cedar Springs, Michigan	**Kevin B. Smith** World War II Veteran Canton, Michigan	
John F. Devries World War II Veteran Grand Rapids, Michigan	**George W. Irvine** World War II Veteran Cadillac, Michigan	**Richard L. Nietert** World War II Veteran Novi, Michigan	**Robert B. Spencer** World War II Veteran Jackson, Michigan	**Deanna M. Hilbert** Trip Leader Rochester Hills, Michigan

Chris Zimmel
Medical Personnel
Clawson, Michigan

Brad P. Ziegler
Official Photographer
West Bloomfield, Michigan

Jeffrey J. Bruss
Trip Guardian
St. Clair Shores, Michigan

Michael Cameron
Trip Guardian
Farmington Hills, Michigan

Mark E. Devries
Trip Guardian
Grand Rapids, Michigan

Melissa Downey
Trip Guardian
Huntington Woods, Michigan

Timothy Downey
Trip Guardian
Huntington Woods, Michigan

Robert C. Gould
Trip Guardian
Ann Arbor, Michigan

Debi Hollis
Trip Guardian
Royal Oak, Michigan

James C. Johnson
Trip Guardian
Royal Oak, Michigan

Debra K. Lee
Trip Guardian
Farmington Hills, Michigan

Gary Lillie
Trip Guardian
Dexter, Michigan

Barbara L. Peluso
Trip Guardian
Troy, Michigan

Gary A. Rutherford
Trip Guardian
Cincinnati, Ohio

Thomas Smith
Trip Guardian
Canton, Michigan

John E. Sullivan
Trip Guardian
Royal Oak, Michigan

"Today the guns are silent. A great tragedy has ended. A great victory has been won. The skies no longer rain death – the seas bear only commerce – men everywhere walk upright in the sunlight. The entire world is quietly at peace.

– General Douglas MacArthur

Honor Flight 32 Saturday, May 8, 2010
More photos of this trip at www.honorflightmichigan.com

Emerson B. Andrews
World War II Veteran
Jackson, Michigan

Alvin J. Evans
World War II Veteran
Troy, Michigan

Ralph J. Koll
World War II Veteran
Grand Rapids, Michigan

William A. O'Dell
World War II Veteran
Hubbard Lake, Michigan

John P. Voss
World War II Veteran
West Branch, Michigan

William C. Bauer
World War II Veteran
Novi, Michigan

John N. Galopin
World War II Veteran
Southfield, Michigan

Hubert J. Kress
World War II Veteran
Houghton Lake, Michigan

Andrew J. Ponstein
World War II Veteran
Hudsonville, Michigan

_____

Pasquale Bucalo
World War II Veteran
Clinton Township, Michigan

George W. Hanka
World War II Veteran
Warren, Michigan

John E. Laidlaw
World War II Veteran
Westland, Michigan

John R. Popovich
World War II Veteran
Commerce Township, Michigan

Richard P. Sage
Trip Leader
Royal Oak, Michigan

R.Arthur A. Camirand
World War II Veteran
Bay City, Michigan

Richard T. Huggler
World War II Veteran
Alpena, Michigan

John M. Madison
World War II Veteran
Charlevoix, Michigan

John Potter
World War II Veteran
Grand Rapids, Michigan

Roderick McPhee
Medical Personnel
Farmington, Michigan

Frank A. Cwik
World War II Veteran
Clinton Township, Michigan

Kenneth W. Jacobson
World War II Veteran
White Lake, Michigan

Frederick W. May
World War II Veteran
Farmington Hills, Michigan

Donald Riggins
World War II Veteran
Westland, Michigan

Brad P. Ziegler
Official Photographer
West Bloomfield, Michigan

Merlin E. Damon
World War II Veteran
Chesterfield, Michigan

Robert R. Kassin
World War II Veteran
Shelby Township, Michigan

Philip J. Michael
World War II Veteran
St. Clair Shores, Michigan

Joseph F. Starosta
World War II Veteran
Troy, Michigan

Joann D. Beste
Trip Guardian
Warren, Michigan

Donald K. Dandrow
World War II Veteran
Wayland, Michigan

Earl F. Kittle
World War II Veteran
Houghton Lake, Michigan

Edward Milewski
World War II Veteran
Clinton Township, Michigan

Norbert T. Starr
World War II Veteran
Troy, Michigan

Steven D. Beste
Trip Guardian
Warren, Michigan

John J. Engels
World War II Veteran
Millington, Michigan

James E. Knaus
World War II Veteran
Grosse Pointe Farms, Michigan

Clayton W. Nickerson
World War II Veteran
Kalamazoo, Michigan

Alex A. Syper
World War II Veteran
Detroit, Michigan

Sandra L. Blossom
Trip Guardian
Vassar, Michigan

Karen L. Cameron
Trip Guardian
Farmington Hills, Michigan

Michael McCarthy
Trip Guardian
Southfield, Michigan

Janet Williams
Trip Guardian
Royal Oak, Michigan

Michael Cameron
Trip Guardian
Farmington Hills, Michigan

Tom C. Moares
Trip Guardian
Davenport, Florida

Pamela S. Carnaghi
Trip Guardian
Troy, Michigan

Gilbert T. Monroy
Trip Guardian
Jackson, Michigan

Diana I. Fahey
Trip Guardian
White Lake, Michigan

Evan K. Schwab
Trip Guardian
Dearborn, Michigan

Roberta M. Hanka
Trip Guardian
Warren, Michigan

William Schwab
Trip Guardian
Dearborn, Michigan

Catherine A. Kavanaugh
Trip Guardian
Dearborn, Michigan

Lon J. Shook
Trip Guardian
Commerce Township, Michigan

Robert J. Kress
Trip Guardian
Attica, Michigan

Norman L. Shook
Trip Guardian
Commerce Township, Michigan

Curran McCarthy
Trip Guardian
Royal Oak, Michigan

Kevin A. Syper
Trip Guardian
Livonia, Michigan

> "Each and every World War II veteran has earned the right to visit the Memorial in Washington, D.C. erected to honor their brave and selfless service to our country. It is our obligation to take them there."
>
> – Dave Cameron
> Founder of Honor Flight Michigan

Honor Flight 33

Saturday, May 22, 2010

More photos of this trip at www.honorflightmichigan.com

In Memoriam

The United States of America has never been a country dedicated to or steeped in the tradition of warfare. Americans, by nature, are not pure soldiers, as some societies have bred throughout history. Americans have always prided themselves on the strength of their character and on the capable skills of the everyday person. The fibers of the American flag are made from the uniforms of laborers, inventors, entrepreneurs, dreamers, workers and intellectuals who all have had a hand in building this country from the ground up. America was founded on the principles of equality and hard work and as a sanctuary for the common good. And, perhaps, it is these qualities that drive the everyday person, who when called on to defend that which he and those before him have built, helps turn a group of proud anonymous individuals into some of the finest soldiers in the history of combat. Nowhere has this tradition been more evident than during the darkest days of the Second World War.

Sixteen million men and women from across the United States answered their country's call during America's involvement in World War II. Without exception, recruitment centers from coast to coast saw their registration books fill with the names of those willing to risk their lives to defend everything that America stood for. Four hundred thousand of those men and women didn't find their way back to the shores of the land they set out to defend. And of those who survived the war, many with physical and mental disabilities, less than five million would have had the opportunity to visit the long overdue memorial built in their honor, at the heart of the National Mall in Washington, D.C.

It is unfortunate that the phrase "freedom is not free" has become somewhat of a cliché in recent times. However, it remains a very important and poignant point because quite simply, freedom is not free. Freedom is not a blessing or right granted unto the American people by a divine power. Freedom is an opportunity bestowed upon us by generations that have come before and were willing to risk everything they had to preserve everything we now enjoy and ultimately take for granted. They gave up the very freedom they were defending just to ensure it was there for the rest of us and for that, we are forever in their debt.

Time has a way of turning realities into myth. American history is full of giant statues of legends who single-handedly shaped the world we live in today. Sixty-five years ago, 16 million American legends set out to save the world and succeeded. Though many of their individual stories of valor may be lost to history, the selfless effort they put forth in service to the American ideal cannot and must not be forgotten. We, as the generations that have come after them, can keep the spirit of their service alive by honoring those who have risked everything for us, by working tirelessly to better the America that they fought to preserve. They fought for the America they believed in and then came home and built it into the most powerful nation on the planet. These men and women are not just our fathers, mothers, grandfathers or grandmothers. These men and women are the embodiment of what it means to be an American and what it means to be a hero.

Honoring the legacy of the greatest generation of Americans goes far beyond that of simple brick and mortar. America loses 1,500 of its best soldiers with the passage of each day. The future of America now lies in the hands of those whom these men and women raised and nurtured to carry her flag proudly. And with whatever the future may hold, whatever path we may decide to take, we must remember one simple thought: we are here, because they were here. And in remembering that, we remember them, and thank them always.

Gabe Downey

— LETTERS FROM OUR VETERANS —

As an ex-GI, I never experienced a finer day than my Honor Flight. The respect shown to us by the Board Members and the Guardians was something I will never forget. The care given Vets who found it difficult to get around was fantastic. The greetings and applause at the airport were breathtaking. Thank you for a wonderful trip that I will always remember.

Sometimes life delivers experiences too overwhelming to adequately express one's gratitude. My trip to Washington, D.C., courtesy of Honor Flight Michigan, was one such experience. Sixty years after World War II, to realize that an organization, such as yours, cares enough to remember those that committed to the defense of our great land is almost a greater reward than our original victory.

While a simple "Thank You" seems totally inadequate, please accept mine and please continue to remind all veterans, and their families that their efforts were not in vain and will long be remembered.

It is with deep appreciation I thank all those involved in the Honor Flight Michigan for my trip to Washington, D.C. To provide this wonderful opportunity to my fellow veterans and myself to see the World War II Memorial and Arlington's somber beauty will never be erased from memory. The warm love, compassion, and helpfulness shown to us by the Guardians was beyond belief. The applause, handshakes and the people thanking us for our service was heartwarming to all of us.

My heartfelt thanks to Honor Flight Michigan for providing this amazing and memorable gift to all of us World War II veterans. It was most generous and compassionate.

Honor Flight Michigan's team of volunteers are truly American heroes to all the vets who had their dreams of visiting the World War II Memorial made a reality. For making my dad's dream come true I am truly grateful.

"I was Remembered and Honored" aptly described the 15 hours I was privileged to spend in the care of Honor Flight Michigan. It is a day I will carry with me always. God bless those of you at Honor Flight Michigan for a job well done – above and beyond the call of duty.

I want to express my sincere thanks for affording me the opportunity to participate in this wonderful program you have created. I truly enjoyed everything about the trip and especially the heartfelt greetings we received at both airports. Just standing at the Memorial and meeting with Senator Bob Dole was a momentous occasion and brought back many memories.

Please express my gratitude to all those from Honor Flight Michigan who were involved in my trip to Washington, D.C. From start to finish this was a most memorable experience and one I will treasure always. As the day passed, I could not help but think of my fellow soldiers who lost their lives in service to our country so many years ago and the others who did not live long enough to see their memorial built. I salute and honor them.

When we arrived in Washington, D.C. and walked into the terminal, the welcome and "Thank You for Your Service" by most everyone in the terminal was quite an emotional and moving experience. The tears were everywhere. As veterans, we have never been thanked for membership in the armed forces like that— EVER. WOW!

What a day! What a GREAT DAY! I will be grateful for my remaining days to all of you at Honor Flight Michigan. Our Guardians were just great – so kind and friendly. May God love you all.

Supporters – Sponsors – Friends

American Legion Frank Wendland Post 253

Brad Bobkin

Boy Scout Troop 1322
of the Great Lakes Council, BSA

C Moon Productions

Chinn Jewelry

The Clock Specialist

Coffee Beanery – Berkley, Michigan

Country Fresh Products

Cub Scout Packs 1604, 1607, 1095, 1628

Daily Tribune Newspaper

The Detroit Free Press

Detroit Legal Imaging

Jim Domanski

Gabe Downey

Elks Club – Royal Oak, Michigan

Engraving Specialists

Esurance

Gallery One

Golden Limousine Service

Grigg

Hollywood Markets

Holiday Market

Jane & Frank Warchol

Jimi's Restaurant Royal Oak, Michigan

Lily's Seafood

Magic 105.1

Jon Mellow

Jeff Miller

National Coney Island

Pronto Restaurant & Catering

Pure & Simple Solutions, L.L.C.

Royal Oak Neighborhood Schools

Jack Salter

St. John Providence Health System

St. Mary's Parish and School, Royal Oak,
Michigan

Stanley Thomas Associates Inc

Staub Financial

Still Life Films

Bill Thomas

UFCW 876 – Madison Heights, Michigan

Uncle Ray's Potato Chips

VFW Acorn Post 1669

WJR News Talk Radio

Wright & Filippis

Yankee Air Museum

— Share Your Legacy for Generations to Come —

Walk of Honor Brick Pavers

Legacy Documentary DVD

3D Rendered Concept Image

— THE LEGACY MEMORIAL —

In an effort to continue our tradition of honoring Michigan's World War II Heroes, Honor Flight Michigan is proud to announce The Honor Flight Michigan Legacy Project.

The Legacy Project is a series of unified media and community efforts aimed at funding our ultimate tribute to every single Michigan World War II hero - a permanent monument in Royal Oak, Michigan, the birthplace of Honor Flight Michigan.

To help fund our planned memorial we will use proceeds from the sale of this commemorative book and sales from our full-length Legacy documentary DVD, which features never-before-seen film of actual flights and interviews with many Michigan World War II heroes. It includes appearances by General Colin Powell, Senator Bob Dole, Honor Flight Michigan Board Members and a tribute to our founder, the late Dave Cameron. In full HD, this film tells the story of how a few ordinary people who were dedicated to a common purpose, chose to say thank you to a generation of true American heroes, Michigan's World War II veterans.

Another important memorial fundraising program is our "Walk of Honor" brick paver walkway leading up to the permanent monument at our memorial. You, your family, your organization, your business, your place of worship, civic group, club or non-profit organization can forever be part of the history of this memorial by purchasing a personalized brick paver. There are many sizes to choose from to make it affordable for all.

Honor a veteran, a family member, a teacher, an accomplishment, a sports team, a friend, a lost pet, a volunteer, a hero, a Scout troop, a school or university. Highlight or recognize your business, a non-profit organization or civic group with a beautiful permanent engraved brick paver on the Walk of Honor at Memorial Park, Royal Oak, Michigan. The park has significant importance in the history of Honor Flight Michigan and to those World War II veterans we served, as it is located directly across Coolidge Highway from the parking lot where the first Honor Flight Michigan trip originated on a cool Saturday morning, April 21, 2007.

We believe this memorial will remind generations to come of the importance of the service and the sacrifices made by all Michigan World War II veterans.

If you would like to make a donation to the Honor Flight Michigan Legacy Memorial, you can send a check made payable to Honor Flight Michigan and mail to:

Honor Flight Michigan
P.O. Box 237
Royal Oak, Michigan 48070

If you would like more information or are interested in purchasing an Honor Flight Michigan Legacy Project commemorative book, Legacy documentary DVD or a brick paver (honoring someone special in your life) for our "Walk of Honor" at the new World War II memorial, please visit our website at www.honorflightmichigan.com or call Melissa Downey at 248-541-1576.